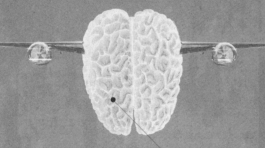

# Holy Wow

## Boost Your
## Youth Ministry Creativity

### Jeff
### WHITE

# Group

Loveland, Colorado

# Group resources actually work!

This Group resource helps you focus on **"The 1 Thing™"**—a life-changing relationship with Jesus Christ. "The 1 Thing" incorporates our **R.E.A.L.** approach to ministry. It reinforces a growing friendship with Jesus, encourages long-term learning, and results in life transformation, because it's:

**Relational**
Learner-to-learner interaction enhances learning and builds Christian friendships.

**Experiential**
What learners experience through discussion and action sticks with them up to 9 times longer than what they simply hear or read.

**Applicable**
The aim of Christian education is to equip learners to be both hearers and doers of God's Word.

**Learner-based**
Learners understand and retain more when the learning process takes into consideration how they learn best.

**Holy Wow**
**Boost Your Youth Ministry Creativity**
Copyright © 2004 Jeff White

Visit our Web site: www.grouppublishing.com

## Credits

Editor: Kate S. Holburn
Creative Development Editor: Dave Thornton
Chief Creative Officer: Joani Schultz
Copy Editor: Loma Huh
Art Director: Granite Design
Cover Art Director/Designer: Jeff A. Storm
Cover/Photo Illustration: Jeff A. Storm
Print Production Artist: Granite Design
Interior Illustrator: Scot A. McDonald/Granite Design; © ArtParts p.6
Production Manager: Dodie Tipton

Unless otherwise noted, Scripture taken from the *Holy Bible*, New Living Translation, copyright © 1996. Used by permission of Tyndale House Publishers, Inc., Wheaton, Illinois 60189. All rights reserved.

Library of Congress Cataloging-in-Publication Data
White, Jeff, 1968-
    Holy wow : boost your youth ministry creativity / by Jeff White.--1st American pbk.
    p.  cm.
Includes bibliographical references and index.
ISBN 0-7644-2667-2 (pbk. : alk. paper)
1. Church work with youth. 2. Creative ability. I. Title.
BV4447.W533 2004
259' .23--dc22
                                                                            2004004524

10 9 8 7 6 5 4 3 2 1     13 12 11 10 09 08 07 06 05 04

Printed in the United States of America.

## Dedication

For my wife and best friend, Amytee

## Acknowledgments

This book would not be possible without the enthusiastic and savvy guidance of my editor, Kate Holburn. Kate knows youth ministry inside and out, and transformed these pages from a jumble of ideas into a cohesive guidebook. I'd also like to thank the following superheroes for their support and insight: Thom and Joani Schultz, Bryan Belknap, Jonny Baker, Jim Burns, Chris Hill, Larry Lindquist, and Mikal Keefer.

# Contents

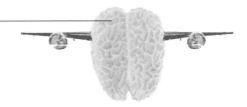

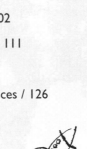

# Introduction

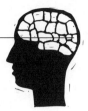

## Be Prepared

I'll tell you upfront that this book contains the information you probably expect it to contain, and hopefully more. But before you jump in, I need to give you a few…um…"warnings."

## Warning 1

Don't read this book.

You're holding this book in your hands because you care about youth ministry. You care about teenagers. You want to help them grow in their relationship with Jesus Christ. So, for their sakes, don't simply read this book…

*Do* this book. Try it out. Play with it. Experience it.

But please oh please don't merely *read* it, since this book is useful only if it's lived out. I'm sorry to say it's rather worthless if you don't put it into practice. If this book were a medication, it would say, "Use only as directed." Otherwise the side effects are not pleasant.

Each chapter includes activities and practical applications that will help you be more creative in your youth ministry. The "Don't Just Read It. Do It!" section helps you experience what you've just read. The "Boost Your Creativity *Now*" section gives you innovative exercises that strengthen your creative muscles and help you apply the book's principles to your youth ministry. "Case Studies" give you powerful examples of real ministries and people who are applying holy wow principles and seeing amazing results.

Do these activities! Some are fun. Some are hard. Some might annoy you. Some will inspire you. But you really should try them out. I promise they will make you a more creative and effective youth worker. Really.

## Warning 2

This book is not about creativity.

It's ultimately about Jesus Christ.

*Holy Wow* was written with one purpose: to give youth workers new creative tools to help students become fascinated with Jesus—a genuine, long-lasting fascination that's healthy and contagious.

Jesus is the way, the truth, and the life. That should be enough to keep us digging deeper for the rest of our lives. And it should be more than enough to keep us pushing creativity to its limits till our last sparking neuron.

Yes, this book is about creativity, but not for the sake of creativity. So if you don't care about helping teenagers grow in their relationship with Jesus, go to amazon.com and find something else. A cookbook maybe.

## Warning 3

This book will not solve your problems for you.

But *it will help you find new ways to solve your own problems*. In other words, *Holy Wow* gives you the tools to create your own solutions for your individual, unique youth ministry challenges.

You won't find shortcuts in this book. It doesn't show you the easy way out. But it does give you very effective ways to be very effective. It offers you a sound, reliable (and fun) strategy for building the spiritual growth of your youth.

I'm writing with the belief that youth workers in general are already an especially creative bunch. But I'm making a promise that your youth ministry will be better after reading (and doing) this book. Why? Because it's designed to help you as a youth worker (whether a novice or a veteran) discover something unexpected and create new ideas in ways you haven't before. It should take your creativity to a higher level.

This is essentially a how-to book—how to inject newness and spiritual fascination into everything you do as a youth worker. It can be done. And in Chapter 1 you'll find out why it *must* be done.

## Warning 4

This book will twist your brain.

There's not much more I need to say about that.

## Warning 5

My mind is a noisy, messy place.

This book has a lot of useful information, and for the most part it's pretty well organized. But it's written from experience, and experience isn't always neat and tidy. Hopefully I've managed to stitch together an accessible volume of new ideas that will prove valuable to you.

You can find books about creativity that are more in-depth, more informative, more fun, more scientific, and yes, more creative. You can gain a lot from those books, and I've even recommended a few of them in Appendix 2. However, all those other resources lack the specific elements essential for practical creativity in the world of youth ministry. An excellent book on creativity in business or the arts is great for business or the arts. Creativity in youth ministry—especially today's unique ministry challenges—needs its own guidelines and direction.

Great creativity is great creativity. But in order to be truly effective in leading teens to transformed spiritual lives, you need the tools from the right viewpoint. *Holy Wow* brings you that perspective from someone passionate about creativity *and* ministry.

## Expect the Unexpected

Don't expect to find gimmicks to make your youth group the coolest, or to achieve the highest levels of genius or perfection. Not in this book. *Holy Wow* unveils powerful, significant ways to helps students draw closer to God…in every aspect of your ministry.

What *is* a "holy wow"? When you discover new, fascinating information, you say things like

◑ "Wow, I never thought of it that way!"

◉ "Wow, that really changed my thinking!"

◓ "Wow, I'm absolutely amazed by that!"

◒ "Wow, can I do that again?!"

When you experience a "holy wow," you're taking a remarkable step forward in your relationship with Jesus. You're finding another reason to be fascinated with your Savior. If that's not worth pursuing, I don't know what is.

This book is about why you need to put holy wow into everything you do, and how to do it.

And I hope you have a lot of serious fun along the way.

"Intelligent people are always open to
new ideas.
In fact, they look for them."

Proverbs 18:15

# Chapter 1

## Invisible? Or Memorable?

People are busy—in fact, busier than ever in history. Like stars in the sky, countless opportunities sparkle for our attention. Everything shouts for our time, our money, and our energy, and they're not all bad options. But somewhere along the way, the church has become just another star in the sky.

Many teens are too distracted to pay attention to the powerful truth the church has to offer. But don't blame the teenagers. And don't be too quick to point a finger at the church, either. The church is one of many voices competing for their attention. Young people today have nearly endless choices, and far less time to sort them out. Every part of our culture is shouting at them, and being chosen is no easy task. Among these countless choices, it's easy for the church to be missed. The church, by not being remarkable to very many people, has become invisible to too many.

### The Sad Truth

Of course, this is bad news. But worse still is the fact that the many teens who *have* chosen to give some of their attention to their local church may be coming away empty-handed. A Gallup study revealed that only 13 percent of Americans have what might be called a "truly transforming faith."

While many youth groups are bursting at the seams in attendance, too many are not effective at building a "truly transforming faith." Do they stand up to Paul's standard in Colossians 1:28? We want to present them to God, perfect (or mature) in their relationship to Christ.

Here's the sad truth about growing just about any youth ministry:

▶ Many teens may not consider you or your ministry a priority in their lives. They have too many other things to choose from.

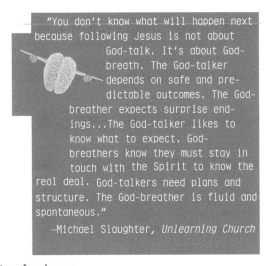

"You don't know what will happen next because following Jesus is not about God-talk. It's about God-breath. The God-talker depends on safe and predictable outcomes. The God-breather expects surprise endings...The God-talker likes to know what to expect. God-breathers know they must stay in touch with the Spirit to know the real deal. God-talkers need plans and structure. The God-breather is fluid and spontaneous."

—Michael Slaughter, *Unlearning Church*

⊙ If teens do decide to give you some time during the week, often it's only an hour or two of their partial attention.

❹ If you do grab their attention, they're likely to forget what you've told them within a few hours.

⊛ If they happen to remember a fraction of what you've told them, they're typically not equipped to apply it to their lives.

❼ And among the small percentage that are applying some biblical truth to their lives, a much smaller number are spreading it to other teenagers.

How many youth within your reach are actively living out and spreading the gospel? How many have a truly transforming faith?

## The Misguided Debate

To break through the clutter of voices and choices luring teenagers, many youth ministries have sought to balance entertainment with biblical education.

The popular philosophy has gone like this: "Teach the teenagers the Bible, but make sure they have fun in the process." Just about everything—Bible studies, worship, mission trips, you name it—has been measured through an enjoyment filter. To grab teenagers' attention, you've had to entertain them.

Teenagers *want* to have fun. And the church has obliged them.

Many church leaders decry the decline of biblical literacy and knowledge among younger generations. Rightly so; many teenagers don't even know what they believe, or why. But the leaders are pointing fingers at the wrong culprits.

The debate shouldn't be about entertainment versus biblical education. We ought to be discussing (loudly and openly) the differences between ineffective instruction and truly life-changing instruction.

We need to approach this subject with honesty. What most people call "solid biblical teaching" usually involves nothing more than pedantic lectures and forgettable chitchat.

Faith that's not lived out is dead. Students are transformed by the truth only if they have a chance to *live* it. Are we truly helping students experience and live out their faith?

"Young people will not develop a conviction that something is true until they live it out in their experience."
—Josh McDowell

Youth ministry should be all about growing a relationship with Jesus. That's what holy wow is all about—engaging teenagers with substance and spiritual fascination.

### Homogeneity Must Die

So how do we engage them?

Society is too noisy and too crowded for the church to be homogeneous. Despite the distractions, teenagers today are too satisfied with their own choices for you to assume you can get their attention. Not being *fascinating* is the same as being invisible. Being invisible is being irrelevant. And if you're irrelevant, you might as well pull up a nice, cozy chair next to your tombstone.

"One-size-fits-all has become one-size-fits-no-one because it was meant to fit everyone."
—Ron Martoia

We absolutely must *individualize, customize,* and *personalize* our youth ministries—even deeper than we think we already are.

Paul didn't use the same approach with every new town in his mission field. Jesus used a wide variety of individualized methods for the different people he encountered. If ever there were two prime examples to follow for customizing your ministry, who could argue with Jesus and Paul?

"Formula" ministry isn't likely to work anymore. To achieve a holy wow, it's absolutely necessary to customize your own unique youth ministry.

### A **Revolution**ary Assertion

It is useless to use average, conventional ministry with today's teenagers. The "proven" methods no longer work. They cause invisibility.

Yes, you'll find many youth leaders who claim legitimate success with traditional, mass-appeal ministry methods. After all, it worked for much of the last century. But the facts are too overwhelming to ignore. Too many teenagers are indifferent to God's Word, the church, and their relationship with Jesus Christ. Many youth workers are working harder than ever, yet not experiencing much fruit from their labor.

If you can't imagine a ministry in which teenagers are fascinated by Jesus, you need to spend your time and money creating something different, something truly new. If your ministry isn't memorable, it's time to change.

You *can* break through. How? By being creative. When you're able to create new, memorable experiences for your youth's specific needs—and generate a holy wow response—teenagers will spread it to other teenagers. You can develop new relationships, programs, and activities that teenagers will actually go out of their way to seek out.

> "Just imagine," cried Mr. Wonka, "...you'll be sitting at home watching television and suddenly a commercial will flash onto the screen and a voice will say, 'Eat Wonka's chocolates! They're the best in the world! If you don't believe us, try one for yourself—now!' And you simply reach out and take one! How about that, eh?" "Terrific!" cried Grandpa Joe. "It will change the world!"
> —From *Charlie and the Chocolate Factory* by Roald Dahl (published by the Penguin Group)

We don't have to reinvent the content itself. God's Word offers enough material to explore for a hundred lifetimes. Our aim is to create new applications and experiences of the content. The containers may change, but the content doesn't.

Since Jesus is the wow of wows, our awesome role is actually to help people be wowed.

In the next few chapters, I'll show you wholly how.

### Case Study: Breakthrough

One of the best holy wow examples comes from a group outside the United States. Hong Kong's Breakthrough Youth Village is one of the most innovative—and effective—ministries in the world.

Though this very savvy organization produces movies, Web sites, books, magazines, camps, even action figures, their focus remains on relationships. Philemon Choi, a founder of Breakthrough, says, "We cannot just communicate with youth through the media. It has to be life touching life."

How many large companies do you know that have teenagers living and playing in their corporate offices? How many top-rated multimedia corporations have you heard that evangelize through "gospel camps" and daily one-on-one conversations? Breakthrough Youth Village does all this, and so much more.

Hong Kong faces a variety of unique challenges within its culture—a Chinese people recently released from British sovereignty and into communist China's rule. Breakthrough couples its evangelistic messages with efforts to help teenagers understand their cultural identity. By caring about current and local social issues, the staff at Breakthrough builds teenagers' confidence by helping them discover their spiritual identities and solve real problems.

These teenagers have become salt and light to the entire community, and the community responds. When Breakthrough sponsored a New Year's celebration, they required young people to demonstrate that they had done a "positive act" in order to gain admission. Thirty thousand showed up. Choi explains why: "People come to us and they are blessed."

Typical youth ministry? No way. Holy wow? One hundred percent.

## Don't Just Read It. Do It!

### HOW ARE yOU DOiNG?

**Materials Needed:** Pen or pencil
**Estimated Time:** Five minutes

Complete the following evaluation to take an honest look at how effective your ministry has been. Every youth worker should ultimately and sincerely answer this question: *Is my ministry truly helping teenagers build deep and lasting relationships with Jesus Christ?*

Circle the answer that most accurately describes your regular youth ministry.

**1.** How often do you or another leader talk one-on-one with most teenagers in your group?

A. I talk with most students usually once a week.

B. I talk with most teenagers at least once or twice a month.

C. I have a handful of teenagers I talk to all the time.

D. My face-to-face conversations are random.

**2.** How often do you or another leader pray about concerns/needs with a teenager or small group of teenagers?

A. Usually at least once a day.

B. A couple times a week or more.

C. Whenever a need arises.

D. We're lucky if we pray for our pizza.

**3.** How many of your students can remember what Bible lesson you studied last week?

A. I'm very confident most of them remember.

B. I'd guess about half of them, give or take.

C. Honestly, probably only a few.

D. How am I supposed to know?

**4.** How much do you follow up on whether teenagers applied what they've learned during your Bible studies?

A. We usually have a thorough follow-up; teenagers share the results.

B. We usually ask a couple follow-up questions in small groups.

C. We ask a couple follow-up questions; one or two teenagers usually answer.

D. We don't usually follow up.

**5.** How often does your youth group personally interact with the community?

    A. We intentionally try to make it a habit.

    B. We schedule special outreaches and events.

    C. We interact occasionally.

    D. We do our best to protect the teenagers from influences outside the church.

**6.** How much of your youth ministry is intentionally geared toward helping teenagers grow in their relationship with Jesus?

    A. Most of it; if it doesn't bring them closer to Jesus, we try not to do it.

    B. Quite a bit; we try to balance the fun and the Jesus stuff.

    C. I probably don't think about it as often as I should.

    D. I'm just happy when they show up.

**7.** How often are most teenagers in your group "wowed" by a spiritual experience?

    A. We try to make it happen often—every week, if possible.

    B. If it can happen once or twice a month, we're happy.

    C. It's not too common—maybe a couple times a year.

    D. My teenagers just aren't "wow-able."

**8.** Does your youth ministry have a plan to reach the "hard" teenagers in your group?

    A. You bet—it's an integral part of our culture.

    B. Whenever possible, we identify them and try to meet their needs.

    C. We try the best we can, but they're hard for a reason.

    D. We treat all teenagers the same.

**9.** Do the teenagers in your group feel comfortable at youth meetings?

    A. We do everything we can to make every kid feel valued and loved.

    B. Most of them do, but someone's always going to be unhappy.

    C. I'm not sure; I hope so.

    D. Learning about God has nothing to do with comfort.

**10.** How much time do you spend being creative?

    A. I need to be creative at least a few hours a week.

    B. I'm busy, but I try to do something creative every week or so.

    C. Being creative is a luxury; I'm lucky to get a couple hours a month.

    D. I don't have a creative bone in my body.

*How to figure your score:* No need to add, multiply, or divide; this book is shooting for straight A's. It might sound idealistic (*might?!*), but we need to aim for the best standard. Anything less is not as effective. And be encouraged, because *it can be done.*

# THE DIFFENDOOFER CHURCH

**Materials Needed:** A copy of the book *Hooray for Diffendoofer Day!*

**Estimated Time:** Fifteen to twenty minutes

Time to flex those creative muscles (and have a little fun in the process). Go find yourself a copy of the book *Hooray for Diffendoofer Day!* by Dr. Seuss, Jack Prelutsky, and Lane Smith. It's a wonderful story about an offbeat, unconventional school. Read it once (just to enjoy it), then read it again—but this time, read it as if you were reading about a church. Then consider the following questions:

1. What kinds of subjects would a Diffendoofer church teach? Think of at least three.

2. What kind of character traits would the leaders in a Diffendoofer church be known for? Do you think those traits would be suitable in a youth ministry? Why or why not?

3. Name some aspects (if any) of your youth ministry that might be more likely to be found in Flobbertown.

4. What specific qualities make a Diffendoofer church different from a Flobbertown church? Name five.

5. In what ways could your youth ministry be more Diffendoofer-like? In what ways could it be less like Flobbertown?

# Chapter 2
## The "New" Creativity

Back in the old days, the best way to get a new idea was to brainstorm. You sat at a table (with or without a small group), then solved a problem by squeezing as many ideas out of your head as possible. Ouch.

There were rules to this barbaric torture procedure:

1. Think up as many ideas as you can, no matter how stupid they are.
2. Write them all down. (Did someone bring one of those big sketch pad thingies?)
3. Criticize your list with a sadistic fervor.
4. Pick what's left.

Sometimes people would try to make this brainstorming process easier to swallow. They added donuts and coffee. Or pizza. Perhaps they made everyone wear a different hat. Or used scented markers. Maybe they sat on beanbags. Some especially bold ones might have taken their meeting outside. But it still quacked like a duck.

The problem with what most of us call "brainstorming" is that it's more storm than brain. While it's good and healthy to work out our mental muscles, brainstorming serves to barrage and drain our minds rather than to open them up and free their potential. Or didn't you notice how tired you were at the end of your last brainstorming session?

Of course, it would be wrong to say the traditional methods never work. Many great ideas have been birthed in deadly dull, formulaic brainstorming meetings. But why go through a creative process that's more like having a baby than conceiving a baby?

There's a much better way.

Getting teenagers' attention in our noisy culture *requires* creativity. What's more, the necessity to individualize and customize your youth ministry demands a deeper and more effective level of creativity—a new creativity—holy wow creativity.

## What Holy Wow Creativity is Not

To understand how top-level creativity works, it's important to deconstruct misconceptions about it. Let's make it clear that holy wow creativity is *not* formulaic, linear, or predictable.

### Creativity *Is Not* Formula

Formulas are great for accounting or production lines, but not for innovation. Formulas are designed to give you the same result time and time again. Formulas take you where you expect to go. Creativity pushes us beyond what we already know.

Don't expect to think outside the box, because there is no box. You can't break the mold because there's no mold to be broken. You can't color outside the lines because…yep, there are no lines.

Formula = box. Formula = mold. Formula = lines.

I doubt many youth leaders would describe their ministries as formulaic. But how many of them take the same ingredients, the same process, the same sameness, and do it over and over?

We can do better than homogeneous, formula ministry. And we can do better than homogeneous, formula creativity.

### Creativity Is *not* Linear

Commonly misused creative methods take you from step A to step B. It's a linear process. It's mathematical. It's logical. It typically produces preconceived, expected results. Even the "mind map" method—which was an inventive departure from typical list-making—is largely linear.

How many thousands of youth workers follow the expected, linear path when trying to create dynamic programs? Let's say you're in charge of next weekend's youth worship service. You're supposed to put together the list of songs, prayers, and so on. Doing this should involve creativity, but how do most folks solve it? Point A, meet point B. I think I'll C you later.

Maybe you're the type who likes to mix it up a bit. You gather a small group together for a brainstorm session. You say enthusiastically, "Let's think up some new ideas for next weekend's youth worship service!" After a half-hour of squeezing how-abouts and what-ifs out of your heads, you might or might not have a great idea. Either way, the process was probably linear, and often predictable.

Samuel Taylor Coleridge described creativity as the "willing suspension of disbelief." When we're being creative, we're going places that just don't make sense to the rational mind. We're connecting the dots that nobody had thought of connecting.

I've heard too many people say, "I can't be creative. I can't even draw a straight line."

Great! The only straight line we want is the narrow one that leads to God's kingdom.

### Creativity Is Not Predictable

When we describe something as "creative," we're typically talking about how "different" or "unexpected" it is. It seems new and fresh, maybe even a bit odd. We were probably surprised by it.

Creative *things* are not predictable; neither is the *process* for creating them.

Stumbling on a good idea is a lot like expressing an emotion. You can't force a genuine feeling at will. It's a response to a stimulus. I can't just tell you, "Be angry!" and expect you to react automatically. I can't ask you to be sad and weepy at 2:30 tomorrow afternoon. It's not likely to happen.

For most people, creativity is not a spigot you can turn on and off. It has to be stimulated. It has to be fueled, just like a genuine emotion. That's not to say you can't be creative whenever you want to. You just have to know how to fire up the sparks that make it happen.

A great creative process *must* expect the unexpected, because we're not looking for a predictable result. Think of it this way: If your creativity produced what you expected, did you even need creativity to get you there?

It's helpful to further understand what creativity *isn't* by looking at its opposites:

- ◗ Creativity is the opposite of convention. Established conventions exist to re-create the same thing consistently and with preconceived results.

- ◔ Creativity is the opposite of repetition. Redundancy is not fresh, new, or original.

- ◖ Creativity is the opposite of destruction. To kill, hurt, tease, ridicule, tear down, oppress, or fight is to oppose creativity.

- ◓ Creativity is the opposite of inertness (or apathy)—in other words, doing nothing and going nowhere.

To clarify this even further, let's also understand what are *not* opposites of creativity:

○ Creativity is not the opposite of reverence. Being creative doesn't mean we have to ignore or break from everything good that's already been established. Creativity definitely goes beyond tradition, but it's not diametrical to spiritual rituals, authority, and biblical standards.

⊙ Creativity is not the opposite of boring. Ironically enough, the process of creativity can sometimes be tedious and wearisome. What's most important is that great creativity be effective on some level. Just because something seems boring to one person doesn't mean it's not creative.

▷ Creativity is not the opposite of order. Much of the creative process described in *Holy Wow* does, in fact, seem disorderly—but it all has a goal, a purpose, and a general set of rules.

## What *Holy Wow* Creativity **Is**

Why do people get great ideas while they're in the shower, driving their car, sleeping, or eating at a diner ("Quick, get me a napkin!")? Because of the very nature of an original thought—it's unlikely to be found where you'd normally expect it. Otherwise someone would probably have thought of it already. These circumstances are certainly outside any formulaic approach. Ideas generated in unexpected, unusual places are unexpected and unusual.

Holy wow creativity thrives in this kind of stirring climate. When you operate within a process that imitates (or, better yet, exaggerates) these circumstances, you significantly increase your creative capacity.

"Different isn't always better, but the same is **never** better."
—Artist James Christensen

More simply: You can eat at Al's Creativity Diner any time you want, and there are napkins aplenty.

Holy wow creativity is not formulaic, not linear, and not predictable—it's *random*, *spontaneous*, and *unpredictable*. For this kind of creative process to work, we need to intentionally foster the right kind of mind-set and environment that fuel it.

To understand this better, do this quick exercise:

Don't Just Read It. **Do It!**

## DEFINING WOW

**Materials Needed:** Paper and pen, Bible, thesaurus

**Estimated Time:** Ten minutes

This quick exercise helps you think about what a holy wow might look like in your ministry. You'll discover a deeper meaning for the holy wow concept.

**1.** Write down ten synonyms for the word *holy*.

**2.** Write down ten synonyms for the word *wow*.

**3.** Mix and match them in new combinations, such as "righteous delight" or "pure wonder."

**4.** Consider the following questions:

▸ Have you ever had a "wow" spiritual experience? How was it different from other spiritual experiences? What kind of effect did it have on your life?

▸ In what ways do you think a "holy wow" experience might be different from "formula" spiritual experiences? Why?

## Creativity Is Random

With formula chained to the doghouse, true nonlinear creativity is free to roam. It's not logical. It's not mathematical. It's rather irrational and nearly chaotic. But the results are dazzling. Therefore, randomness is a crucial factor in the brilliance of creativity.

Despite humankind's attempts to create linear systems in everything we do, those systems always blaze their own unpredictable trails. The examples are infinite—think of any humanly developed system, and you'll likely discover random variables that changed it as it developed. A person invents something amazing, and immediately everyone attempts to harness and control it. Yet, as this new system runs its course, it repeatedly surprises us. Why? Because that's how God created it to work.

This is why the traditional brainstorm method falls short. It doesn't create a stimulating environment. It's restricting. It's not random. It's too much formula.

Obviously, thousands of youth workers have conceived effective ministry ideas through a traditional creative method. But I'm willing to bet that a majority of those great ideas were probably sparked by something random, spontaneous, or unexpected that "accidentally" leaked into their process, whether they knew it or not. Somehow, great creativity happened *in spite of* the method. It snuck in, wreaked its wonderful havoc, then snuck out.

Once and for all, let's dispense with the subterfuge.

If you intentionally foster a holy wow creative process that includes randomness, you're *much* more likely to generate great ideas, get lots more of them, and have a better experience in the process.

"...there are no rules here—we're trying to accomplish something."
—Thomas Ediso

How can we ensure stronger creativity? Let the process surprise you. Because it probably will.

### Creativity Is Spontaneous

Intentional accidents. Cultivated improvisation. Synchronized disorder.

These are just different ways to describe holy wow creativity's necessary element of spontaneity. Does it sound contradictory? Yes, and beautifully so.

If a nonlinear process is to produce unexpected results, the process needs to be haphazard and unpremeditated at some level.

Larry Lindquist understands. Although he's a nationally respected youth leader, at heart he's just a guy who cares about teenagers' relationship with Jesus. He relates one story:

"I remember speaking at a senior high winter camp in northern Wisconsin. It was incredibly cold that night. I had prearranged with the camp director to have a bonfire all ready to go. In the middle of my talk on evangelism, I had the students grab their coats and race to the bonfire. They quickly huddled around the fire in a tight circle. It was quickly obvious that if they didn't back away and sacrifice some of the warmth, there were some students who would be 'left in the cold.' I drew their attention to the parallel to their world at home. They understood and the point was frozen in their memory."

What a great example of spontaneous, creative thinking! I asked Larry how he was able to think of such a great object lesson on the spot. His response: "I'm not really sure." He says he doesn't consider himself an especially creative person (he should give himself more credit). But he describes his youth ministry process as "chaperoning a dance between creativity and risk." He does this by testing acceptable boundaries in his own realm of creativity.

### Creativity Is Unpredictable

"If you can tie something very unexpected (even strange) with your point, it will be remembered far longer," says Larry.

Larry's nailed it, in both his creative process and his intended effect. Even when he's not conscious of it, he's using randomness and spontaneity to produce unexpected—and *memorable*—results.

Many of the activities you'll experience in this book include "intentional accidents." When you actively participate in the exercises, you may do some things that, in and of themselves, may not make much sense. Perhaps they seem too random, chaotic, or unpredictable. But when you follow through, it's the end result that will surprise you—and often present a list of ideas you would have never thought of otherwise.

Don't be afraid to let your creative thinking be too crazy or fantastic, just because you're not sure of what the outcome will be. It's a lot easier to scale back a wild idea than to think of a brand-new one.

## Why Does Holy Wow Creativity Work?

It's all about *discovery* and the first-time experience.

They're things you never forget: The first time you tried sushi. The first time you flew in an airplane. The first time you kissed someone. The first time you attended a professional sports game. The first time you saw your favorite movie. The first time you got a paycheck. The first time you went snorkeling in the ocean. The first time you fiddled with the ring on your finger and thought, "I'm actually *married!*" You can probably think of a hundred of your own "firsts" in ten minutes or less.

Remember: The ultimate goal of holy wow creativity is to create new ways to help teenagers grow in their relationship with Jesus.

Not only do you remember these times in your life, but you also remember the intimate details: the emotions, colors, sounds, smells, and the people who were involved. First-time experiences define the word *memorable*.

There's something exhilarating about the raw, genuine joy of discovery. It drove Columbus to America and sent people to the moon. And whether you realize it or not, it's what drives teens to your youth group. They want to discover God…over and over.

Discovery can also be experienced as "ah-ha!" moments—points in time when the light bulb flashed on and you "got it." They make you feel smarter, wiser, more complete. I believe the wisest people have the most "ah-ha!" moments.

As it relates to ministry, holy wow creativity emphasizes newness by re-creating the first-time experience. It's compelling because it's a discovery. A first time. An "ah-ha!"

## Free Indeed

Creative freedom has to be nurtured and protected, because it doesn't happen automatically. You have to be intentional about it. Sometimes you have to fight for it (righteously, of course). Above all, we have to be

Christ-minded about it. When Christ sets us free, we're free indeed.

When Jesus said we need to have the faith of a child to enter his kingdom, he spoke volumes about the very nature of Christianity. A child's faith is pure, totally trusting, and virtually unlimited. Children utterly believe in the impossible. Jesus went so far as to say that if we don't have the faith of a child, we can't enter the kingdom of God (see Matthew 18:3-4 and Luke 18:16-17).

Are we willing to "suspend disbelief"—just like a child—for the sake of discovering something that will wow us?

### So Far, *So Good*

To create holy wow after holy wow after holy wow in your youth ministry, you need to be able to generate a wealth of great, original, new ideas. Let's sum this up quickly and simply:

○ In order for the church not to be invisible to youth in our culture, we need to help make a relationship with Jesus fascinating to them.

● To sustain this fascination, we need to be highly creative in inventing new, memorable ways of experiencing a relationship with Jesus and remembering God's truth.

◐ To be highly creative, you need to support an atmosphere and a process that fuels creativity to happen.

⊙ To set up the ideal process for creativity, you need to understand how to use the right elements, including randomness, spontaneity, and unpredictability.

We'll explore the details of that process in the next two chapters. This party's just getting started.

### Case Study: Blockbusters

Bryan Belknap loves movies. He has an unusual ability to recall even the most oddball details in the films he watches. It's almost scary. But he's no trivia nut—Bryan possesses an incredible capacity to discover moral lessons and character principles in movies most people might never expect. He says his creativity is the "natural result of spirituality." His imagination stays fresh and fueled because he stays in tune with God's truth and is led by God's Spirit.

Bryan's written two great books about finding spiritual lessons on the big screen: *Group's Blockbuster Movie Illustrations* and *Group's Blockbuster Movie Illustrations—The Sequel*. Bryan shows us a perfect example of someone who creatively (and brilliantly) applies his passion for youth ministry within a relevant cultural framework.

If you take a closer look at how Bryan relates the Bible to the cultural media that's engaging teens today, you'll know right away he doesn't shy away from the truth. Yet he doesn't back down from appreciating and understanding the greater world of art and imagination.

Bryan doesn't separate creativity from his relationship with Christ. "If I close myself off from creativity (which is all from God, even if it's sometimes warped by someone's broken relationship with God), then I'm missing an opportunity to reach people with the gospel."

Well said.

Get a wealth of more creative and useful insights at Bryan's Web site: www.ministryandmedia.com.

## Boost Your Creativity NOW

### INFINITE ALPHABET

**Materials Needed:** Seventy-eight index cards, pen or pencil, notepad, Bible

**Estimated Time:** Flexible—thirty to ninety minutes

Here's a great practical activity that puts the principles of randomness and unpredictability into action. Just as the twenty-six letters in the alphabet can be arranged into a great number of combinations, any other set of single ideas can be combined into a vast number of greater ideas. I recommend doing each step before moving on to the next step.

1. Write down twenty-six physical features of your church or youth ministry on twenty-six index cards. (Physical features include items like a set of floor cushions, a door, or a candle, as well as places like the kitchen or hallway.) Next, write twenty-six kinds of activities, events, or programs on twenty-six new cards (for example, communion, leader training, or talent night). Then write twenty-six spiritual topics (such as servanthood, God's power, or fasting) on twenty-six more cards.

2. On the other side, label the cards in each group from A to Z. (Each card should have a feature on one side and a letter on the other.) Keep each pile of twenty-six cards separate.

3. Take a piece of paper and write down twenty to thirty three-letter words.

4. For each three-letter word, select a lettered card from each of the three piles. (If the word is "cat," select the "C" card from one pile, the "A" card from another pile, and so forth.) Pick one combination of three letters and move on to step 5. (Note: Since letters such as Q and Z aren't used in many three-letter words,

you may also randomly select a card from each pile.)

5. The three cards will reveal an unexpected combination of ideas (like "stool," "prayer meeting," and "peace"). Think of at least three ideas from this combination and write them down. Then move on to the next three-letter word and repeat the process.

Some combinations won't amount to anything significant, but some will open your eyes to ideas and insights you haven't thought of before.

**Take It Deeper:** Think up your own varia-tions of the card piles. Perhaps you might include names of students in your group, names of songs, or outreach opportunities.

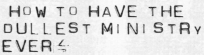

Don't Just Read It. **Do It!**

## HOW TO HAVE THE DULLEST MINISTRY EVER⁴

**Materials Needed:** Pair of scissors or a razor blade

**Estimated Time:** Five minutes

Here are a few handy suggestions that are guaranteed to bore your teenagers into a state of mental rigor mortis and cozy spiritual lukewarmness. Please read the following list, then follow the instructions on page 28.

### Rules for a Deadly Dull Youth Ministry:

1. Do the same activities over and over and over and over and over and over and over and over and over and over again. After all, repetition is the next best thing to redundancy.

2. Make your prayers long and pedantic. If you don't know what *pedantic* means, just keep praying until you make yourself weepy.

3. Do nothing but read the Bible to your youth group, especially several chapters at a time. Nothing screams, "Teach me more, please!" like a pair of glazed eyes.

4. Do everything yourself. Remember, two people mess things up twice as much as one person.

5. Who says no one ever laughs at old jokes? Keep telling them; the students are probably laughing on the inside.

6. When a student guesses a wrong answer, teach them the fine art of looking sheepish. It's what separates humans from the animals. Except the sheep.

7. Restrict snacks to animal crackers and watered-down Kool-Aid. Teenagers' nostalgia for kindergarten Sunday school will surely respark their love for Bible learning.

8. Tell your students lots of stories about your childhood. Since they're not likely to have had one themselves, they'll be very curious to hear about all the original experiences that made you so clever.

**9.** If you're truly serious about changing lives, just keep flashing them your old WWJD tattoo.

**10.** Trick them into thinking it will be better next week. Like the old saying goes, "Fool me once, shame on you. Fool me twice, shame on you some more, and so on and so forth."

**Instructions**

A. Cut or tear this page out of the book. **Really.**

B. Place this page in a folder labeled "ZZZZZZ."

C. File the folder in the back of your filing cabinet.

D. Don't ever look at it again.

# Chapter 3

## The SHINE Mind-set

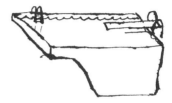

I hate getting into a cold swimming pool.

The best way is to hold your breath and jump in. Before you know it, the shivers are over and your body adjusts. But what do I normally do? I take the stairs into the shallow end. Step by freezing step. It's stupid, I know. It's a mental thing—the anticipated horrible icy shock and imminent hypothermia never really happen. It's all in my mind. For me, jumping in requires more than an attitude adjustment or change in perspective. If for only a brief second, I need my entire mind-set to change in order to take the plunge.

What's *your* cold swimming pool? What does your brain tell you is more difficult than it actually is?

Problem solving and creative thinking are definitely cold swimming pools for a lot of people. Revolutionizing your youth ministry in a way that gets teenagers fascinated with Jesus may seem more like an Arctic Ocean ice hole.

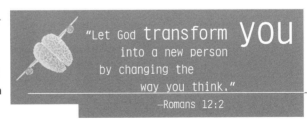

"Let God transform you into a new person by changing the way you think."
—Romans 12:2

Your attitude is a critical part of whether or not this kind of creative process will work for you. Holy wow requires what I call the SHINE mind-set—a set of values necessary to use the holy wow creative process. Yes, there are other important mental and spiritual characteristics, but these five are the most crucial.

## S—Start With the Savior

The purpose for this book is to help you wow students with Jesus Christ. As I mentioned earlier, *Holy Wow* isn't ultimately about creativity as much as it's about students growing in their relationships with Jesus.

As followers of Christ, our mind-set during the creative process—whether for generating ministry ideas or personal endeavors—should honor Christ and bring us closer to him. Original creation began with Christ (Colossians 1:16-17), and we should pursue all creativity through Christ. Because in him we live and move and exist (Acts 17:28), and apart from him we can do nothing (John 15:4-5).

Jesus himself shines as an amazing example of creativity. When we "start with the Savior," we follow his example (1 John 2:6).

The activities and exercises in this book are specifically designed to drive you in the direction of God's kingdom. As you generate new ideas, keep in mind how those ideas might affect teenagers' relationships with Jesus. As you sort through which ideas to use, consider how it might open their eyes to significant truths about Christ. And as you apply the ideas to your ministry, aim for experiences that fascinate teenagers with Jesus. Read 2 Corinthians 5:13-15, and let those thoughts guide you.

Remember this, too: As you create new ideas for your youth ministry, how will they bring *you* closer to Jesus? Your relationship with the Savior is just as important. Jesus ought to be *your* wow of wows, too.

## H—Humble Yourself

Creativity has nothing to do with making you look good.

It's so easy to become prideful when you think of a really great idea. I'll be honest—I've let it happen more than I'd like to admit. It goes to your head faster than you can say, "cometh before the fall." Pride is deadly and can eventually destroy your ministry, not to mention the devastation it can wreak on others. C.S. Lewis called pride the most dangerous of sins. Remember, it's what got Lucifer into all that trouble.

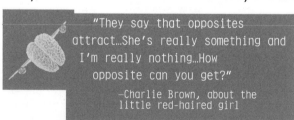

"They say that opposites attract...She's really something and I'm really nothing...How opposite can you get?"
—Charlie Brown, about the little red-haired girl

Besides, humility has such tremendous power. Being humble brings us grace (James 4:6), God's presence (Isaiah 57:15), and makes us truly great (Matthew 18:4).

A lack of humility affects your creative honesty, as well. If you want *your* idea to win out in a group, you're not allowing what could be the *best* idea to have a chance. Your judgment becomes severely impaired. I guess you could say friends don't let friends drive creative sessions with pride. Think about others before yourself (Philippians 2:3-4).

This humbleness applies to your willingness to submit your preconceptions to the creative process too. Holy wow creativity will lift you to new heights, but not if you're the boss. You have to admit upfront that you don't have the answers (yet), and that you're going to allow the Holy Spirit to lead, let the process run its course, and see what happens in the end.

You will benefit greatly; just remember that it's not about you. Submit yourself to God, give credit to God, honor God alone.

Consider this: The root word of humble is *humus* (Latin), which means soil, dirt, ground. *Humus* is where seeds grow…so perhaps humility is where creativity can best grow?

## I—InvOlve Others

Creativity is not for mavericks.

What's better: a solo home run, or the grand slam? Better yet: a game well-played by one person and lost, or a game won? Alone, you'll fall short, period.

Many of the activities you'll do in this book are exercises you can do very effectively by yourself (some of them you *should* do alone). But most of them will produce better results when done by two or more people together. You may do some part of the creative process on your own, but you need to involve someone else at some other point—even if it's just to get feedback on your ideas. This principle is explained in depth in Chapter 8.

Since this is all about Jesus Christ, we need to remember the concept of the church body. "What a strange thing a body would be if it had only one part!" (1 Corinthians 12:19). The parts of this body depend on others (Romans 12:5), and together they bring God's providential presence (Matthew 18:19-20).

"The wise are glad to be instructed, but babbling fools fall flat on their faces" (Proverbs 10:8).

Just think of creativity as a team sport. Youth ministry analogies to golf are apt to be sub-par anyway. (Sorry...)

## N—Newness Rules

Whenever you're doing a creative exercise, you're looking for the fresh and the original.

Consider these Scriptures:

- "Sing *new* songs of praise to him" (Psalm 33:3).

    - "Those who become Christians become *new* persons…A *new* life has begun!" (2 Corinthians 5:17).

- "You must display a *new* nature because you are a *new* person, created in God's likeness…" (Ephesians 4:24).

❶ *"New* wine must be stored in *new* wineskins…"* (Matthew 9:17).

Jesus Christ is all about newness—new life, a new covenant.

More often than not, "newness" means "new to us"—the discovery or experience of existing truth. That's important, especially as you develop ideas for ever-exploring teenagers.

I love Ezekiel's vision of the valley of dry bones in Ezekiel 37. Imagine the rattling as all those bones came together, the muscle and flesh growing over them like some Hollywood special effect. Then a driving wind blows through the valley, filling the dead bodies with breath and igniting new life. Ezekiel's vision represented God's mercy in giving new life and hope to the exiled Israelites. It can also serve as a vivid illustration of how creativity can give new life to old ideas.

Most human creativity is an adaptation of something that's already been created. Newness doesn't have to be absolutely brand-new-and-never-been-done-before. Just remember there's a difference between adaptation and cloning.

I'll say it again: There is no magic formula you can do again and again to invent great ideas. Your mind-set, from beginning to end, should be to endeavor to find the new idea. If you generate a list of ideas that don't pass the newness test, change them. Then change them again. That first-time experience is a powerful thing.

Avoid the "stagnant quo." Repetition kills holy wow creativity. Cloning is not allowed. Think fresh.

## E—Experience It

"Do, or do not. There is no try." —Yoda in *The Empire Strikes Back*

Yoda was no youth pastor, but he understood the power of experience.

The ideal mind-set for jumping into creativity must involve a willingness to get your hands and feet dirty (literally). Creative *theory* is for college. You've got to put holy wow into practice.

You must get out of your brain cage and put your whole self into the creative process. "Hands-on" isn't a catchphrase—it's absolutely critical. This element of the SHINE mind-set is just as important as the others. And if you don't do it you deserve a kick in the SHIN.

Christ's great commission tells us to "*go*" (Matthew 28:19). We know we're supposed to be doers and not only hearers (James 1:22). Ecclesiastes 12:11 tells us, "A wise teacher's words spur students to action." I repeat, *action*.

An easy analogy: Do you try new foods by reading cookbooks? No, you get in the kitchen and get busy.

So don't just sit there…

## Jesus **SHINEd**

People point to Jesus as a premier example for a lot of things: his teaching style, his leadership approach, his communication methods. Maybe somebody out there is teaching people how to fish like Jesus.

I'll follow the crowd here. But at least I can confidently state that Christ embodied creativity. Besides having a hand in the creation of the universe (Colossians 1:16-17), Jesus was inventive and original—he did unexpected things:

▶ When Peter asked Jesus about taxes, Jesus told him to go catch a fish and pull a coin out of its mouth. (Matthew 17:24-27)

⊙ When Jesus healed a certain blind beggar, he wiped spit-mud in his eyes and told him to go jump in a pool. Nice. (John 9:6-7)

▼ When the Pharisees asked Jesus about the adulterous woman, Jesus scribbled in the sand. It's not important *what* he wrote, but the fact that he did it at all. (John 8:8)

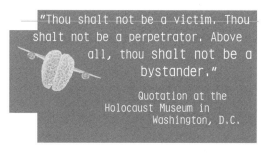

"Thou shalt not be a victim. Thou shalt not be a perpetrator. Above all, thou shalt not be a bystander."

Quotation at the Holocaust Museum in Washington, D.C.

Jesus' most often-used creative skill was storytelling. Mark 4:34 tells us that when Jesus appeared in public, he never talked about anything without telling a story. You can be sure he was very good at it.

Jesus also lived out genuine creativity in his original ideas, metaphors, and miracles. It's important to remember, though, that everything Jesus did was with a purpose.

Above all, Jesus always had the right attitude. He's the living example of all the SHINE traits: He came to be our Savior (Matthew 18:11) He remained humble, though he had a billion reasons not to be (Philippians 2:7). His entire ministry was about involving others (Mark 1:17). He makes all things new (Revelation 21:5). And, no doubt, Jesus was the preeminent doer.

Go and do thou likewise.

## SHINE OUT LOUD

**Materials Needed:** Six music CDs, headphones, paper, pen

**Estimated Time:** Thirty to forty-five minutes

This exercise is an enjoyable demonstration of the principles of randomness and unexpectedness. It forces you to create ideas you probably wouldn't have generated otherwise.

**1.** Think of one youth ministry topic or challenge you'd like to solve (for example, a worship theme, a missions fundraiser, or the topic of forgiveness). Write it at the top of your page, then forget about it.

**2.** Find six CDs, each with a different music style.

**3.** Randomly pick a number between one and nine (provided each CD has at least nine songs on it). This number will be the track you listen to on each CD. For example, if you picked a three, you'll listen to track 3 on all six CDs.

**4.** Wearing your headphones, listen to each selected track for about two minutes. As you listen, write down four or more words that come to mind. For example, if you're listening to a jazz tune, you might write words like *chase, slither,* or *horn.* Some words may pop into your head that don't seem to make any sense at all; write them down. Do this for all six tracks.

**5.** Select one of the six CDs (preferably one with a more ambient style) and let it play in its entirety as you work on step 6.

**6.** For each descriptive word you've written down, think of how it might work together with the ministry challenge you wrote earlier. Force yourself to think of at least two ideas for each word. For example, if you've written down the word *brick,* and your challenge to solve is a study on forgiveness, think of what forgiveness might be like if it involved a brick.

**7.** You should end up with about fifty ideas, and hopefully more. Most of them will not be useful, but some of them will be. The goal is not to think up fifty fascinating ideas; you only need one. Choose the top three that seem to be the most interesting and flesh them out—work with them for a few more minutes until one of them gets you close to a holy wow.

**Connect It to Your Youth:** Before your youth meeting, think of a topic such as pain, love, or friendship. Give each student a pen and paper. Play portions of three very different songs and give students a couple minutes to write down at least three nouns that come to mind as they listen to each song. Then have them discuss in small groups how some of their words might serve as metaphors for the main topic. (For example, if a student wrote down the word *garbage* on their list, they could describe how friendship can sometimes feel like taking out the garbage.) Have a few of them share with the entire group after a few minutes.

Boost Your Creativity NOW

## THEM BONES

**Materials Needed:** White paper, scissors, tape, markers

**Estimated Time:** Twenty to thirty minutes

**Connect It to Your Youth:** Ahead of time, cut thirty-seven "bones" out of white paper (you'll be constructing a life-size skeleton). Talk with your group briefly about the valley of bones in Ezekiel 37:1-14. As a large group, have the students help you think of thirty-seven things that, as with the Israelites, might separate them from God and make them like dead bones. Have students write each thought on one of the paper bones and gradually construct the entire skeleton by taping each bone to the wall. Then have students meet in small groups to discuss specific ways God can breathe new life into their dead bones.

# Chapter 4

## Give Me Oil in My Lamp— Creative Catalysts

Creative blocks *itch*.

And it's like you've forgotten how to scratch. You sit at your desk, or pace back and forth, racking your brain for a new idea—a brilliant solution that will make everyone say, "ah-ha!"

But it doesn't come, and you settle for an *OK* idea, often out of mere mental exhaustion. "Oh well, at least it's not a *bad* idea," you console yourself.

The well-trained pros (and the lucky few prodigies) know how to break those creative blocks with ease. But most of us common folk have had plenty of times when our minds go blank. You might stare at your computer screen for ten minutes and not even realize it. Your head could feel so numb you barely remember your name. Sometimes drool is involved.

It's like having sand in your shorts. It distracts you so much you can't think about anything else. What you need is a shower.

A catalyst shower.

You *can* tap into greater brain-power. Creativity requires it without exception. You need a booster for your rocket. Cheese for your mouse-trap. Oil for your lamp. Fortunately, the resources for doing this are readily available. This chapter will show you how to do it.

> "We are not as strong as we think we are."
> —Rich Mullins

If you want to shine, you need the fuel.

Let's get this fire started.

## Catalysts

An ideal creative atmosphere has a variety of catalysts that serve the purpose of turning the key in the ignition of your mind. Catalysts offer four incredible benefits.

▶ *Catalysts literally stimulate your brain, causing it to be more active.* A stimulated mind is much more capable of thinking of new ideas than an idle or cluttered mind. Catalysts help clear your head of the cobwebs, making you more alert and aware.

⊽ *Catalysts expand the range of ideas your mind can access.* The right kind of catalysts help you break outside of your known world and open up unfamiliar and unexpected information. They give you a bigger pool (hopefully not a cold one) to dive into.

● *Catalysts help you stay energized.* It's hard to be creative when you're mind is going blank, you're tired (mentally or physically), or you're having trouble staying focused. Certain catalysts give you energy, get your blood pumping, and give you a second wind.

⊙ *Catalysts provide inspiration.* Sometimes all you need to keep going is something that encourages you. Catalysts motivate you to dig deeper into your mental reserves than you thought possible.

University studies have shown that using catalysts in creative sessions not only works, but works better than anyone expected. In one study, researchers took groups of college students and gave them the exact same assignment—to think of ideas for new snack food products. Half of the groups got a room, chairs, paper, and pens. The other groups got the same, plus some catalysts such as music, magazines, toys, and other physical objects. The catalyst groups tended to think of ten times as many ideas as the other groups.

One of the primary reasons traditional brainstorm sessions aren't as effective is because they typically lack any catalysts. People are told to "bring their thinking caps," and nothing else. It's kind of like inviting your entire church to a potluck and bringing only plates and napkins.

God's blessed us with a wide variety of catalysts, including play, environment, music, physical objects, existing ideas, and personal experiences. Let's take a closer look at each of those.

## *Play*

I've heard several "smart" people scoff at the notion of involving play in "serious" creative efforts. They call it flaky, silly, or even vacuous. They are 100 percent wrong.

Play is a highly effective catalyst that, in simple terms, gets your brain juices flowing. We want the neurons in our brains to be active, and play activates them as well as, if not better than, many academic endeavors. It's widely believed that passive behaviors like watching TV or listening to people talk (that is, lecture) do not help develop the brain, and even serve to slow cerebral activity.

Play is good, and good for you. It gets neurons connecting and gets the blood flowing.

What kinds of play are we talking about? It can be something as simple and subconscious as fiddling with a paper clip, bouncing a ball, or kneading clay. Catalyst play can also include intentional activities like LEGO-building, foam ball battles, or finger puppets. You can find a lengthy "Cata-List" of items in Appendix 3.

> "People whose work is creative self-expression of the most obvious kind—artists, writers, musicians, dancers—seem to be drawing heavily on play to do what they do. What they all have in common is the urge to take what is known and rearrange it in new combinations." —Fred Rogers

Sound childish? That's the whole point.

I guarantee if you set some of these play catalysts out on your conference table before a brainstorm session, two things will happen: First, people will pick them up and have fun with them. Second, the ideas that come out of that meeting will be profoundly better than any ideas they would have without the catalysts.

Play = Catalyst = Brain Stimulation = Better Ideas.


### Environment

For me, environment is perhaps the most important kind of catalyst. Your ability to work, play, create, and relate can be significantly influenced by the atmosphere of your environment.

You only need to follow two general guidelines:

1. Decorate wildly.
2. Change it frequently.

Both guidelines are highly satisfying acts of creativity in and of themselves. They also help you maintain a catalyst environment that fuels your creativity. Don't think of your space as your office; think of it as your creativity studio—your holy wow lab.

A lot of youth workers are very good at this. They rival graphic designers and visual artists for their inventiveness. Their "offices" (and I use the term loosely) are more like galleries of the freakish and bizarre. Some examples:

⊳ A youth room with walls covered with shoes. It's part of an ongoing lesson for graduating students on walking with Jesus.

▽ A windowless youth office painted entirely black as a

dramatic and unforgettable backdrop for illustrating the power of being the light of the world.

⊽ A fish collection of hundreds of items—ceramic fish, papier-maché fish, plastic fish, inflatable fish, you name it. It's meaningful to teenagers because it's a living symbol of how everyone has something to give.

The most important thing to remember about a catalyst environment is that it can be anywhere. You need some kind of home base (a room, office, desk, corner, whatever) to get a lot of your creative work accomplished. Then seek out catalysts in different external environments: museums, bookstores, antique shops, zoos, cafes, cemeteries, galleries, and (especially) the great outdoors.

Even within your church building you can find great locations to stir your thinking. Have a creative session in the baptistery, the janitor's closet, the kitchen, the nursery, or on the roof. There's nothing inherently creative about those locations per se; but they give your brain new connections and add randomness and nonlinearity to your approach.

Your environment is your workshop—make sure you have the right tools.

## Music

No catalyst offers more variety than music. It doesn't matter which type you like; music stimulates brain cells, energizes the mind, and inspires the heart. You can set the volume on low or high. You can use the privacy of headphones or make the room boom with vibrating speakers. Any way you like to do it, it offers the same benefits.

There is no doubting music's powerful influence on the mind. A tormented King Saul was calmed by David's music (1 Samuel 16:14-21). I know some people who like to blast heavy rock music while clearing their heads. Others prefer barely audible worship music in the background. How to use music as a catalyst is really up to you.

For the optimum effect, however, try new music (new to you, at least) for your creative sessions. When the brain hears familiar music, the stimulation is limited because the neural connections follow common pathways. When you introduce fresh sounds, your brain makes new connections and is forced to create new patterns of thinking. New music reinforces the randomness and unpredictability of the creative process.

Your choices are truly unlimited, since it would take a couple lifetimes and a lottery budget to listen to all the recordings out there. The more music you explore, the better a catalyst it becomes. You should especially consider instrumental music or CDs with minimal lyrics. Look for jazz, movie scores, electronica, ambient, world, bluegrass, and anything not already in your collection. Sound effects CDs are great catalysts for group creative sessions.

### Physical Objects

Many youth workers are already avid collectors of random physical objects. They usually have a story behind them, but not always. Their collections might include things like

Jars of hot sauce    A rubber chicken

Candy dispensers

Hawaiian leis

Red superhero boots

Inflatable aliens

Fast-food restaurant hats

Action figures    Teapots

Street signs    Pinwheels    Roller skates    Blank frames

Maracas

Giant-sized crayons

Millions of physical objects just like these are useful for providing a spark in your imagination. Use them in your creative sessions. Mix and match them. Turn them into unexpected metaphors. Take them apart and put them back together. But most of all…

Don't keep them for forever. Recycle them. Throw them away and replace them with new objects. The dusty lava lamp you've had for ten years has got to go. A great rule of thumb is to keep odd objects in your creative space no longer than six months. They have a very short half-life—they lose their intrigue rather quickly. Keep your eyes open for something unique and out of place. Add it to your catalyst menagerie, make good use of it, then donate it to someone else.

In addition to that, start a themed collection. Pick a specific object or subject and see how many variations you can find. It can be just about anything—from crosses or nativities to zebras or toy robots. You'll be amazed at the diversity and originality of what you'll find.

Take care not to place too

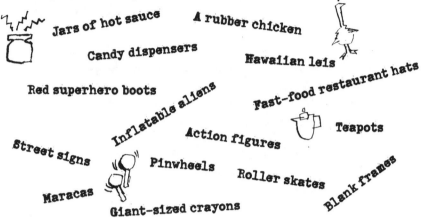

"A fruit or vegetable can look like a mouse or a bear or a human face…It is the miracle of seeing a new truth—one that was there in the first place and needed only your imagination to give it substance."
—Joost Elffers, *Play With Your Food*

much value on physical object catalysts. You *want* them to be temporal. Sure, some things have sentimental value. But your priority sentiments should be focused on finding new ideas to help teenagers become fascinated with Jesus. Separate the eternal from the moth fodder.

### Existing Ideas

Some of the best catalysts for creating Jesus-based experiences are published youth ministry resources. Books, kits, and magazines offer a wealth of ideas already proven to work. Don't just tap into them—*plunge* into them. Use them and abuse them. They're full of great ideas that can spark even more ideas.

Remember, a primary benefit of holy wow creativity is that it gives you the power to invent individualized, customized solutions for your youth ministry's specific needs. Pre-existing idea books are a perfect place to start. Scour them for ideas, then make those ideas your own. (You can find a short list of excellent idea books in Appendix 2.)

Jim Burns is one of the most trusted youth ministry leaders in the country. He's earned that respect because of his genuine passion for reaching teenagers with God's love. When I asked him about creativity in youth ministry, he said communicating the gospel is all about creativity. "We can all be more creative than we are now. We need to stretch, risk, and be exposed to creative ways to make faith come alive," Jim says.

Not only does Jim have a Ph.D. and a national radio program, he's got a solid grasp on creativity in ministry that only comes with years of experience. He understands that reaching your audience in a memorable way requires a catalyst.

Only God can truly create something *ex nihilo*—out of nothing. We humans have to create from that which already exists.

As Jim says, "We aren't talking about plagiarizing, but if someone shares a good idea and it may work for you, then copy it. My best ideas came from someone else—I just adapted it from them."

Jim told me a great example of how he had modified what he'd seen other people do:

"I recently participated in an ordination ceremony and the pastor anointed the head of the new pastor with oil. I took the idea and adapted it for a crowd of five thousand teenagers. After my talk they were invited to be commissioned to serve

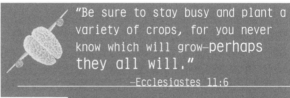

"Be sure to stay busy and plant a variety of crops, for you never know which will grow—perhaps they all will."
—Ecclesiastes 11:6

Christ in their families, communities, and the world. The teenagers came to several stations in the arena and pastors anointed their heads as a commissioning to their commitment. It was very powerful."

It was holy wow.

## Personal Experiences

Places, objects, and other ideas are great catalysts for fueling creativity. So are personal experiences.

Engaging in certain activities can stimulate your thinking and generate those random, spontaneous, and unexpected ideas. Like all other catalysts, experiences stimulate your brain, create new connections, and give you new perspectives. Earlier, I mentioned showers, diners, and short road trips. These are perfect examples, and yet are barely a scratch on the surface. I find artistic activities to be among the most effective, but you can also use everyday experiences and uncommon adventures.

Some artistic examples include:
- Painting (with watercolors, oils, even finger paints)
- Sketching and doodling, especially in new environments
- Playing musical instruments
- Sculpting (clay, papier-maché, wire, and other media)
- Making and painting pottery
- Woodworking
- Writing, especially fiction and poetry
- Paper making
- Origami
- Stage performance
- Scrapbooking

Everyday experiences are particularly valuable because the experience itself can often be mindless or innocuous, allowing your thoughts to wander freely. Some examples include:
~ Walking
~ Yardwork
~ Napping
~ Cooking
~ Cleaning
~ Organizing
~ Painting walls
~ Driving
~ Showering
~ Bike riding

Adventurous activities give your brain intense, new connections, but it's often difficult to sort them out until it's over. Still, they're incredible catalysts for generating fresh ideas. Some examples:
≈ Sky diving
≈ River rafting

∿ Rock climbing

∿ Snowboarding

∿ Skateboarding

∿ Bungee jumping

∿ Roller coaster riding

∿ Gathering street testimonies

And perhaps one of the most moving personal experiences of all:

❖ Silence

The key to making a personal experience an effective catalyst is to have your youth ministry challenge in mind while you're doing it. Or, as a plan B, debrief alone or with a partner immediately following the activity. Better yet, do both.

## How **Big** Is Your Bucket?

Your catalyst reserve is like a bucket. You can fill it with as much as you want. You can make your bucket bigger and deeper. But you can only get out of it what you put into it. It could be said that the most creative people have a catalyst bucket so expansive they can dive in and never touch the bottom.

Take care not to over-

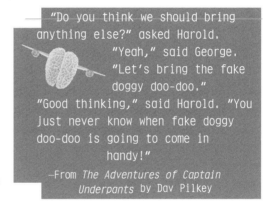

"Do you think we should bring anything else?" asked Harold.
"Yeah," said George. "Let's bring the fake doggy doo-doo."
"Good thinking," said Harold. "You just never know when fake doggy doo-doo is going to come in handy!"

—From *The Adventures of Captain Underpants* by Dav Pilkey

dose on the catalysts when you're using them, however. More (at one time) does not necessarily make merrier. You need to be able to stay focused on the potential solution, and not allow the catalysts to become a major distraction.

Don't Just Read It. Do It!

### BUCKETS

**Materials Needed:** Large bucket or sack, a stack of magazines and/or catalogs, a blank greeting card, scissors, glue stick

**Estimated Time:** Forty to sixty minutes

The creative process is kind of like fishing out of a bucket. You're limited to catching what's swirling around inside. The larger and more filled the bucket, the greater number of ideas you can catch. This moderately easy exercise shows you one way to expand your creative bucket and fill it up. Note: Follow the instructions one step at a time; please don't read ahead.

1. Take your stack of magazines and cut out pages that include images and words you find interesting or eye catching. Don't worry about what you'll be doing with them, just cut out fifty to a hundred pages.

2. Put all the pages into your bucket or sack. Without looking, pull three individual pages out of the bucket.

3. Using *only* the images and words from those three random pages, create an encouraging greeting card for your pastor, fellow youth worker, youth group member, spouse, or friend. Cut out specific images and words with your scissors and glue them to the blank greeting card. Push yourself to think creatively and force a fun solution out of the pages you selected.

**Consider these questions:**

◉ What did you think about the pages you were cutting out of the magazines? What kind of internal filters did you use to decide which pages to keep?

◉ What do you think of the card you made? Would you have ever thought of that combination of images and words on your own?

◉ Try the activity again. Pull three new pages out of your bucket.

**Connect It to Your Youth:** Help your teenagers exercise their creativity with the same activity above. Cut out enough pages ahead of time and place them in one large bucket or sack. Have each teenager randomly select three pages. Instruct them to make an encouraging greeting card for one of the other pastors or ministers in your church. Talk with them about the randomness and unexpected results of their activity, and relate it to how a random and unexpected act of encouragement helps them grow in their relationship with Jesus.

## WONDERMART WANDERLUST

**Materials Needed:** Note pad, pen

**Estimated Time:** Forty-five to ninety minutes

This activity uses the concept of catalysts to spark new ideas.

1. Think of a specific youth ministry challenge you'd like to solve or topic you'd like to creatively tackle (for example, a Bible study about sin and repentance). Write it at the top of your note pad.

2. Walk the aisles of a large discount or drug store. Observe the details of a variety of products and make parallels to your subject. Write down all your thoughts, even if you don't think they might be useful later. (For example, observe cleaning products—what they do, how they do it, what they're contained in, how long they last, and so forth—and write down analogies related to sin and repentance.)

3. Repeat your observations with at least three or four different types of products and relate them all to your primary subject.

4. Buy a pretzel and soda and sit at a little table in the store, if possible, and review what you've written. Look for new thoughts and unexpected connections.

5. How could you relate what you've discovered to your youth? How could you help them experience this topic in a fresh way? Could they interact with any of the products you observed? How can you create a servant-oriented experience based on what you've discovered?

**Connect It to Your Youth:** If any of your observations spark new ideas, be sure to bring and use any relevant products in your activity. Letting your youth physically interact in an object lesson will help them remember it. If the object you choose is inexpensive enough, you may even buy one for each student so everyone can take it home as a souvenir.

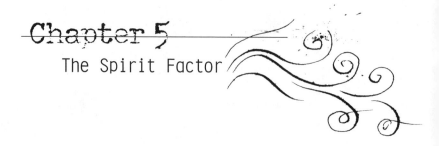

# Chapter 5
## The Spirit Factor

The very first person the Bible mentions as being filled with God's Spirit was an artist.

Not Adam, not Abraham, not Moses, not Joshua, not David.

It was an artist named Bezalel.

The Bible refers to Bezalel as a "master at every craft (*The Message*)." Exodus 31:1-5 tells us God gave Bezalel the skills to "create beautiful objects" (the New International Version says "make artistic designs") with jewels, precious metals, wood, and "all kinds of craftmanship." Bezalel and his team of artists—the Bible calls them naturally talented craftsmen—obeyed God's orders and fashioned a long list of dazzling masterpieces, including the Tabernacle, the Ark of the Covenant, furnishings, altars, accessories, and the "beautifully stitched" garments for the priests.

What a golden age of creativity that must have been!

### God Loves Creativity

Our God is a creative God, no question. His creation reveals barely a glimpse of his brilliance, and we're not even close to grasping the depths of it. He creatively made us in his image and has passed along that attribute to us. The drive to create is part of our nature.

The Bible is full of examples of creative endeavors. Here are a few:

- Cooking (Genesis 40:1)
- Embalming (Genesis 50:2-3)
- Cosmetics and beauty treatments (Esther 12:2)
- Color design (Exodus 25:1-5)

Fashion design (Exodus 28:3-5)
Jewelry making (Exodus 28:17-21)
Perfume making (Exodus 30:25)
Sculpting (Exodus 32:4; Numbers 21:8, 9)
Weaving and tapestry making (Exodus 35:35)
Poetry (Deuteronomy 32:1-43)
Dancing (1 Samuel 18:6-7)
Music (2 Samuel 6:5)
Singing (1 Chronicles 25:1)
Winemaking (Nehemiah 13:15)
Metalsmithing (Isaiah 40:19)
Pottery (Jeremiah 18:3)
Carpentry (Matthew 13:55)
Painting (Jeremiah 22:14)

People used these skills to glorify God. Frequently their creativity was an act of obeying what God told them to do. When they used their creative skills selfishly or in disobedience to God, they paid dearly. Using creativity for destructive purposes brought severe consequences.

Obviously, art has always played an important role in God's interaction with his people, and in our ability to glorify him.

**Bezalel Today**

We find two interesting parallels here for twenty-first century youth leaders:

○ Just as God commissioned Bezalel and others to build the Tabernacle and everything in it, he calls leaders today to build his church (1 Peter 2:5).

⊙ And just as creativity was an essential part of Bezalel's assignment to help bring the Israelites closer in their relationship with God, creativity can boost our calling to help teenagers grow in their relationship with Jesus Christ.

Bezalel honored God, creating everything "just as the Lord had commanded" (Exodus 39:43). And the result? By the power of God's Spirit, Bezalel used his creative artistry to help the Tabernacle to be "filled with the glory of the Lord" (Exodus 40:35).

The account of Bezalel should serve as a great encouragement to us that God cares about using our creative abilities in our efforts to serve him. It's just as relevant now as it was some thirty-five hundred years ago.

**The Holy Spirit Distinction**

I believe the Holy Spirit empowers our gift of creativity.

As followers of Christ, we are blessed by the distinction of having the

Holy Spirit in our lives. We know the Spirit gives us gifts and skills as a means of helping the church (1 Corinthians 12:4-7). The Holy Spirit regenerates (John 3:3, 5), guides (John 16:13), teaches (1 Corinthians 2:10-16), helps (John 14:16-26), bears fruit (Galatians 5:22-23), and more in the Christian's life.

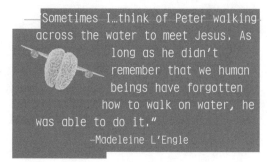

"Sometimes I...think of Peter walking across the water to meet Jesus. As long as he didn't remember that we human beings have forgotten how to walk on water, he was able to do it."
—Madeleine L'Engle

Christ himself was led by the Spirit (Luke 4:1). You could think of *ultimate* creativity as the ability to do the impossible, and Jesus—being fully God and fully human—did impossible things on a regular basis. Christ stated we would do greater works than he did. God calls us to do the impossible, and by his Spirit we can do it. "You...are controlled...by the Spirit, if the Spirit of God lives in you" (Romans 8:9, NIV).

"Now, the Lord is the Spirit, and wherever the Spirit of the Lord is, he gives freedom. And all of us have had that veil removed so that we can be mirrors that brightly reflect the glory of the Lord. And as the Spirit of the Lord works within us, we become more and more like him and reflect his glory even more" (2 Corinthians 3:17-18).

God is the maker of our creativity, the Spirit is the fuel of our creativity, and Jesus is the glory of our creativity.

## Say Yes

When Jesus invited Peter to walk with him on the water, Peter said yes. When the angel Gabriel called Mary with God's message about bearing his son, Mary said yes. When Jesus instructed his disciples to feed five thousand people with a handful of food, they said yes. When Moses instructed Bezalel to construct the most beautiful Tabernacle possible, Bezalel said yes.

Holy wow creativity is an act of incarnation—to personify Christ in what we create. The original incarnation—God become man—is undeniably fascinating. As the disciples spread the gospel, they were continuing the incarnation, making Jesus real to people through their lives and actions. We, too, strive to continue the incarnation of Christ to teenagers. Creativity can

"I was watching you," he said quietly. "I used to pray once. Do you talk to God when you pray?"
"Yes."
"I have lost that faculty. I cannot pray. I talk to God through my sculpture and painting."
"That's also prayer."
—Chaim Potok, *My Name Is Asher Lev*

help us make Jesus real to them. We want young people to be fascinated by Jesus. We want them to say yes to him.

God wants us to be productive, and God will provide the means for us to do it. "For God is the one who gives seed to the farmer and then bread to eat. In the same way, he will give you many opportunities to do good, and he will produce a great harvest of generosity in you" (2 Corinthians 9:10). God also warns us about being idle and nonproductive with our gifts—judgment will come (1 Corinthians 3:10-15).

As the Spirit leads, follow. If God has blessed you with above-average creative skills, use them! Hone them! Maximize them!

## "Pagan" Creativity

So why do so many non-Christians create such amazing things?

Sometimes it seems like the "worst offenders" are the most creative and talented. Some of our greatest artists and creative geniuses seem to have embraced sin with a passion. Why should God bless them with such great gifts?

Two things to remember:

❿ God has given creativity to all humans. When he created mankind in his image, his attribute of creativity was part of the package.

⊽ We're all sinners. We all deserve nothing short of death, much less a gracious gift.

Thankfully, Jesus paid that price for us and we have the chance to enjoy creativity to its fullest and most enjoyable potential.

Those who ignore Christ's redemption look elsewhere. Since many non-Christians have a God-hole to fill, the creative arts become their god. Rather than look to their Creator, they throw their entire lives into their art. They have different reasons—to deal with pain, cause change, or celebrate themselves. This passion, however misplaced, fuels the kind of power and focus needed to create magnificent works of art.

The creative passion and skills of atheists, agnostics, and other seeking souls often far exceed what we see from churchgoing Christians. Why? I believe it's their willingness to question, risk, experiment, doubt, and push limits—things most Christians avoid. You'll find shining lights throughout history, but the majority of "Christian" literature, music, and other art for the past twenty-five years has been substandard. (Maybe I'm being unfair; a good percentage of secular stuff is of low quality too.) But that's a whole other book to write…

Talk to your non-Christian friends about creativity. Better yet, gather a group of nonchurchgoing people in a room and ask them to help you solve some of your youth ministry challenges. I can almost guarantee they'll think of ideas you would have never considered. And this will also provide a great opportunity to show them God's love in a hands-on, humble sort of way.

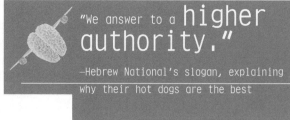

"We answer to a higher authority."

—Hebrew National's slogan, explaining why their hot dogs are the best

Ultimately, being a Christian *should* give us an edge creatively. We have the Holy Spirit. We have an eternal purpose. And we have the greatest motivation. If we're going to fascinate teenagers with Jesus, we need to be fascinated ourselves.

## Case Study: The Labyrinth

London is one of the most toured cities in the world. It's also home to thousands of youth hungry for something spiritual in their lives.

Jonny Baker—a self-proclaimed Londoner, Christian, dad, and director of his own independent Christian record label—is a national coordinator for the Church Mission Society in the U.K. He's been blogging online for years and produces some truly progressive ambient music, but he's also a regular guy who has a sincere heart for spreading the love of Christ to youth.

Not too long ago, Jonny and his friends saw an opportunity to reach people in an amazing new way. Using the beautiful St. Paul's Cathedral, they set up a Christ-based labyrinth in the center of the main floor. Guided by CD with meditations, instructions, and music, visitors walked their way quietly through the labyrinth, stopping at contemplative, interactive stations along the way.

It was worshipful. It was meaningful. And it blew people away.

Word spread. One thing led to another, and Jonny's labyrinth soon became an innovative packaged product called *The Prayer Path*, which makes the labyrinth accessible to churches in the United States and Canada (ministry leaders in other countries can find it as *The Labyrinth* at http://proost.co.uk). More often than not, I've watched teenagers—even the hard, cynical ones—finish their labyrinth experience in tears.

*It's as holy wow as holy wow gets.*

As creative as Jonny Baker is, he doesn't take all the credit. "It arose out of a group of us planning. This is a key thing in the development of creative ideas. Knocking around ideas in a group often produces more than if it's just you on your own."

For a peek into what drives Jonny's passion, visit his blog at http://jonny-baker.blogs.com/jonnybaker. You'll love it.

Don't Just Read It. Do It!

# GOD ENCOUNTER

**Materials Needed:** Note pad, pen

**Estimated Time:** Thirty to sixty minutes

In Jonny Baker's labyrinth experience, visitors encounter God at several stations throughout the path. As they listen to the meditations and music on the CD, they engage in various activities that stir their senses and make the experience more memorable. For example, at one station they give their worries to God while dropping stones in a bucket of water. At another station they consider how their lives affect the world around them as they leave footprints in sand.

Now it's your turn to think of an activity for a single "God encounter" station like those in the labyrinth. You'll be given a specific topical direction and related Scripture. Think of an original, memorable way to experience God through it.

1. Read John 16:4-15 and Galatians 5:22-23. Consider the Holy Spirit's role in our lives—how the Spirit guides us, teaches us, and produces fruit through us.

2. Using a catalyst of your choice, think of a way to demonstrate the concept of allowing the Holy Spirit to produce fruit through our lives. You might consider using things like fresh fruit, scented spray, candles, or something more inventive.

3. Write out ideas for your God encounter, considering how teenagers might walk away with a greater understanding of how the Spirit works in us.

4. Test the idea on yourself, and then on two friends. Get their feedback, make any adjustments, and then retest the idea.

5. Write out instructions for students to follow. Be sure you're specific in your step-by-step directions.

6. Set up your station, with all necessary items and supplies, and let your students experience the station.

## ROAD SIGNS

**Materials Needed:** Bible, thesaurus or other word book, one or more youth-oriented magazines, colored pens or pencils, colored poster board, construction paper, markers, scissors, glue stick

**Estimated Time:** Thirty to ninety minutes

This exercise challenges your creativity and has you come up with new combinations of ideas that you can relate to your relationship with God. It's visual, textual, and puts spiritual ideas in a different context. This activity is most effective with a group of three working together.

1. Make yourself several copies of the road signs shapes on page 53 (opposite).

2. Using your Bible for ideas, create several road signs that serve as scriptural warnings for your youth. Use *one* road signs page as your canvas. (For example, you might write on the stop sign shape, "STOP sinning.")

3. Now push yourself further. Using a thesaurus or other word book, create variations of the warnings. Challenge yourself to fill in *two* whole road sign pages. (For example, you might write on the stop sign shape, "STOMP gossip.")

4. Go further. Using a youth-oriented magazine, create new spiritual warnings that play off popular phrases or slogans. Look for the unexpected, and push yourself to fill in *three* road signs page. (For example, you might write on the stop sign shape, "Don't STOOP to their level.")

5. After you've created at least six full pages of ideas, take your top two or three and create full-size signs to hang in your youth meeting area. Use the poster board, markers, scissors, and glue stick, as needed.

**Take It Deeper:** Keep a couple copies of the road signs page with you for a few days. Look for experiences, conversations, ads, and other unexpected places for new ideas for scriptural warning signs. Sketch them in as soon as the idea comes to your mind.

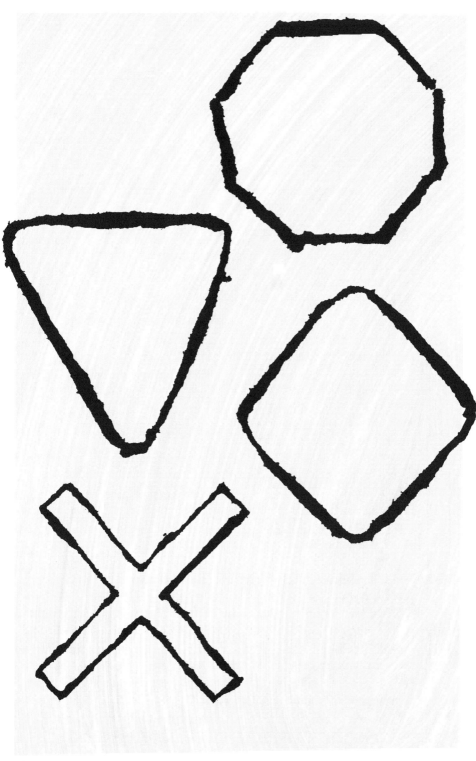

# Chapter 6

## Egg Hatching—The Discipline of Creativity

Horton is a creativity hero.

Dr. Seuss' hapless elephant wasn't a genius. He wasn't remembered for inventing great things or solving impossible puzzles. In fact, he had a reputation for being rather neurotic. People accused him of hearing voices...of having an identity crisis...of being obsessive-compulsive.

Horton was an elephant of perseverance, and his perseverance got him more ridicule than you could shake a truffula at.

In *Horton Hatches the Egg*, the elephant promised to sit on a lazy bird's egg so she could take a break. The bird didn't return, but Horton didn't break his promise:

"I meant what I said

And I said what I meant...

An elephant's faithful

One hundred percent!"

Finally, a miserable year later, the egg hatched. And what came out shocked everyone:

"MY WORD! *It's something brand new!* IT'S AN ELEPHANT-BIRD!! And it should be, it *should* be, it SHOULD be like that! Because Horton was faithful! He sat and he sat!"

Horton's behavior didn't really make sense to everyone else. In fact, it was truly absurd. But he had made a promise to be faithful. His commitment and endurance paid off.

Holy wow creativity requires this kind of nonsensical perseverance. Even if it doesn't seem logical in the middle of all that randomness and unpredictability, in the end you'll be surprised with something brand-new...your very own elephant-bird.

> "On the good days, anyone can be creative. **But** to make a living at it you have to be creative on the days when your dog dies and your tire blows out and your computer decides to imitate both."

## Stick-to-itiveness

It's in the dictionary.

*Stick-to-itiveness* describes creativity's discipline process *perfectly* (and inventively). You have to stay with it...and stay with it...and stay with it...and then...stay with it some more.

Horton stuck to it. Through the freezing winter, the laughter, the fear, the rocky seas, the humiliation—he stuck to it.

Great creativity requires an effort like Horton's. If you're going to be good at it, you need to get used to words like *perseverance, discipline, commitment, determination,* and *diligence.* You must be willing to push yourself past the first fifty ideas and find fifty more. The holy wow process makes it possible, and then makes it probable.

I'm not a body builder, but I read a book about it once. The extremely muscled author, Bill Phillips, described in his best-seller *Body for Life* what it takes to get those muscles into superhuman form. He called it the "level 10 experience." Level 1 is sitting at rest, level 4 might be a brisk walk, and level 6 could be climbing stairs. Most people, even when they're working out, might never get to an 8 or 9. But a level 10 is when you're giving it every ounce of effort you can possibly spare. If you're lifting weights and your body is screaming, "I can't possibly do another!"—do one more, and that's a level 10 experience.

The intensity of a "level 10" is different for everyone. It doesn't matter how much you can handle; to reach a 10 you've got to push yourself beyond what you expect yourself to be capable of.

Hebrews 12:12-13 urges us: "So take a new grip with your tired hands and stand firm on your shaky legs. Mark out a straight path for your feet. Then those who follow you, though they are weak and lame, will not stumble and fall but will become strong."

To get those great holy wow ideas, we often need to reach a "level 10" effort. Just like our muscles, we have to push our brain farther than we think it can go.

In Chapter 2, I referred to the traditional brainstorm session as a barbaric torture procedure. Unlike the holy wow creative process, those brainstorm sessions give you the "ow" without the "wow." It's like trying to build your body by carrying a dead gorilla on your back—it may be possible, but why do it?

The discomfort that comes with a truly effective creative process is a byproduct of stick-to-itiveness. Pushing your mind to a level 10 isn't easy, but it pays off. You can have confidence that the end result will reward your efforts.

## Are You In a Rut?

We get into ruts. All of us. It's essential to being efficient. We create routines and habits that help us save time for our priorities.

That's a good thing.

We also get into ruts in youth ministry. It's also in the name of efficiency. We're so busy from week to week, we teach ourselves to automate certain ministry functions—even things like prayer, worship, greetings, devotions.

That's a bad thing.

If we want to meet the individual needs of our youth, we need to question some of the ruts we've allowed ourselves to fall into. We become "home blind" to our own customs and practices.

Creativity in youth ministry should be all about newness and originality. Don't assume anything. Don't take anything for granted. Redefine *normal*. Grooves are overrated. Even changing some of the smallest habits can open your eyes—and hopefully your teenagers' eyes, too.

### When the Going Gets Tough

Forcing yourself even to begin a creative activity is often half the battle. Pushing yourself to the level 10 experience is the other half of the battle.

You can't just wait for the right conditions (Ecclesiastes 11:4). There's nothing fancy to say about it—you just have to do it. Whether you're just getting started or right in the middle of a creative exercise, you absolutely need diligence and determination to see it through. Maybe you've got a specific challenge and the exercises in this book just don't fit what you need.

If you hit a creative block, here are some suggestions for clearing the cobwebs and finding a new spark:

- Take a quick break. Don't stop entirely, but do something to rest your mind for a few minutes. Go for a short walk, eat a snack, chat with a friend, stretch your muscles, sing a song, shoot some baskets.

  - Find a new catalyst. Go to a new location and find some unrelated physical objects, toys, or sounds.

- Switch contexts. If you're trying to solve a youth ministry challenge, think about how the challenge might be solved in a new context, such as a manufacturing plant, prison, football team, or cruise ship.

  - Reword your ideas. Stop and take a look at the problem to solve or the ideas you've generated so far. With a thesaurus in hand, find at least two synonyms for everything you've written; or rename your original problem.

⊽ Go to a bookstore. It gets your legs moving and offers an ocean of catalysts.

❯ Get your hands working. Fiddle with something tactile to stimulate some brain cells.

⊳ Use a different medium. If you've been writing with pens and paper, try sidewalk chalk, crayons, cereal, or anything else out of the ordinary.

● Think backward. Take your challenge or solution and picture what it might look like in reverse.

⊙ Exaggerate. Think of the problem—what's the worse-case scenario? Think of your solutions so far—what if you took them to extremes?

⊙ Read your Bible. God's Word is always full of wisdom and restores us.

"Imagine how cool Pop Tarts would be if the brand manager was the sort of person who ate them for dinner."
—Seth Godin, Purple Cow

⊳ Meditate. Forget about your activity for a while, close your eyes, and concentrate on God. Use Psalm 77:11-12 as a starting place.

▼ Pray for others. Concentrate for a little while on blessing someone else. Think of someone who needs prayer and ask God to work in his or her life.

❯ Clean. The physical act of tidying up or dusting off is not only a good parallel to clearing your head, it actually does it.

⊽ Exercise. Get your heart pumping and energize your body.

❯ Play a game. Or do a puzzle. Get your mind working in a different direction for a few moments.

● Get a second opinion. If you're by yourself, find someone to bounce thoughts off of. If you're in a group, get an outsider to offer suggestions.

⊳ Sleep on it. Rest up and tackle it the next day.

This is a very short list of possibilities. Creative blocks happen, but they should be overcome relatively easily. Make your own list of inventive block-breakers and tack it to your door.

If you're diligent with keeping your catalysts fresh, you'll struggle less. Throw out old stuff, especially anything you haven't used in six months. And search for new things, particularly whatever you haven't given much thought to before.

## How Far Will You Go?

What if I could guarantee that you could become 500 percent more creative by

- always walking backward,
- sleeping in aluminum foil,
- eating at least seven cans of tuna every day,
- writing only with orange crayons, or
- tattooing your tongue.

Would you do it? Even if it were positively 100 percent guaranteed? How far would you go to become a creative genius?

Here's a more important question: Would you do any of the above if it meant that a majority of teenagers in your youth group would develop genuine, lifelong relationships with Jesus?

Of course, the behaviors above are absurd. They won't help you achieve anything except experiencing the world in a different way. But how far would you go for the cause of Christ? To fascinate teenagers with Jesus, we need to be willing to go to greater lengths—to dig deeper, to think harder, to leap farther than ever before.

If I could guarantee that you could tap into a power that not only makes you more creative, but actually helps teenagers develop a truly transforming faith in Jesus, would you do it?

You don't have to juggle knives or dye your arms blue. But you *must* have the discipline and perseverance to follow and trust God's Spirit. Push yourself to let the Spirit be your power source. Only the Spirit can take you there, anyway.

## Always Be Ready

You never know when some great ideas are going to arrive. You can't always predict where they will come from. But you have to be ready to catch them, net in hand.

"The earth keeps some vibration going
There in your heart, and that is you.
And if the people find you can fiddle,
Why, fiddle you must, for all your life."
—Edgar Lee Masters, *Spoon River Anthology*

In his nonfiction book *On Writing*, novelist Stephen King writes, "Good story ideas seem to come quite literally from nowhere, sailing at you right out of the empty sky: two previously unrelated ideas come together and make something new under the sun. Your job isn't to find these ideas but to recognize them when they show up."

Be vigilant. You already know that ministry can happen at any time—sometimes at the worst times—and you have to be prepared. Creative challenges, too, can come at you out of nowhere. And the solutions can sneak up on you if you're not paying attention. Commit to equipping yourself to discover innovative solutions wherever you are. If you stick to it, your ministry and creativity will work hand in hand.

You can do anything, but you can't do everything. Horton chose the egg. To be productive, choose what's most important to your ministry. You want those ideas to find you. You want that holy wow experience to jump up and spread wings.

You want that egg to hatch.

### Case Study: Workcamps

It all started with a problem.

In 1976, a major flood in Colorado destroyed dozens of homes and killed more than 150 people. The next summer, Thom Schultz, a youth worker who had recently started his own little youth ministry magazine, saw an opportunity. He organized a group of teenagers and spent a week rebuilding some of those homes. They served together during the day and worshipped together at night—a creative combo.

It was such a holy wow experience that they've done it every year since.

They realized the problem wasn't just a local one. Millions of people are either unable or can't afford to make necessary repairs on their homes. Leaky roofs, drafty windows, peeling paint, unsafe stairs—the list of problems was a very long one. So Thom and his team determined to do something about it.

Group Workcamps now sends more than twenty thousand teenagers and their leaders out to dozens of communities around, and outside, the United States every summer. For a week, they get up early to work hard all day, then spend each evening worshipping and creatively experiencing biblical truths. And they grow in their faith every moment along the way.

Talk about discipline. Parents can hardly believe their son or daughter actually worked so hard ("*My child did what?*"). These teenagers persevere through serious labor. They hear the heart-breaking stories of the residents. They sweat, swat bugs, get sore, and spend each night on the floor. And, remarkably, their spirits are renewed each evening with the truth of Jesus' love.

I've had the privilege of volunteering at a few workcamps myself, and I've been blown away each time. I'm always amazed at the excitement and energy the students have, from the moment they arrive 'til their tearful goodbyes.

Thousands of homes get critical repairs, and thousands of people see the light of Christ. Most of all, tens of thousands of teenagers grow in their relationships with Jesus—and they don't forget it.

As Joel Fay, the vice president of Group Workcamps, says, "It's all about spiritual growth." It's all about holy wow creativity.

## Don't Just Read It. Do It!

## RUTS

**Materials Needed:** Ten index cards, hole punch, about thirty feet of cotton string, pen, paper

**Estimated Time:** Part 1: forty-five to sixty minutes; part 2: ten to fifteen minutes

Use this exercise to identify your well-worn habits and try new methods of solving problems. It's in two parts; do part one first. This activity can be done solo or with a partner.

### PART 1

1. Take your index cards and write a behavior you've made into a habit. Follow this format: "When I _____ I always _____." For example, "When I lead singing, I always use my guitar." Write one on each card. Try to think of at least ten habits (they don't have to be bad habits).

2. Punch one hole in each of your index cards, and tie each to the long piece of string. Space the cards at least a few inches apart. Suspend the long string across the room at about chest level.

3. Figure out a different way to detach each card from the string *without* cutting the string. For example, what about using scissors for one and biting off another, and so on?

4. After detaching each card, think of at least three different ways to do the behavior written on it. They don't have to be wild or crazy, just different. Follow this format: "When I _____, I might try _____." For example, "When I lead singing, I might try using a harmonica." Do this for all ten of your index cards.

### PART 2

This section reinforces the concept and gives you an extra creative exercise that's fun and stretches your mind.

1. Think of new word combinations for the acronym RUTS as it relates to routine and habits in your unique youth ministry. (For example: "Rot Until They Stink," "Ride Under The Steamroller," or "Repeat Unoriginal Thoughts and Styles.")

2. Force yourself to think of at least two acronyms. A dictionary or thesaurus is helpful.

**NOW**

# STREAM OF RIGHTEOUSNESS

**Materials Needed:** Paper, pen

**Estimated Time:** Twenty to thirty minutes

This experience forces you to use a stream-of-consciousness approach to answering the questions. Doing this exercise on a regular basis helps you to develop mental discipline and focus. Expect to discover raw honesty and unexpected answers.

1. Answer the following questions one at a time. Answer them by responding with whatever pops into your head—keep it flowing and don't stop. Don't worry about punctuation. Write your answers quickly and without analyzation; don't go back and read what you've already written. Try to stick to the topic, but don't worry if your response makes no sense. Fill up at least one page.

   **A.** What does a friendship with Jesus look like?

   **b.** Why should people give each other gifts?

   **C.** How is the Holy Spirit like the wind?

   **d.** What do you think Christ's crucifixion felt like?

   **E.** What does a lukewarm Christian do on Sundays?

2. After responding to each of the above questions, review your answers. Consider the following questions:

   ❍ What did you write down that you wouldn't have said out loud if someone asked you in person?

   ❍ Did any of your responses surprise you? Why or why not?

   ❍ How well do you think your answers reflect how you honestly feel about these subjects? How well do your answers mirror biblical truth?

**Take It Deeper:** Try the same stream-of-consciousness approach with solving a specific ministry challenge. Set up the activity the same as above, but think of your own specific, open-ended questions. Push yourself to keep each answer running fluidly for five, ten, fifteen minutes. After you're done, review your responses to look for new, unexpected ministry ideas.

# Chapter 7

## 1+1=2—The Science of Creativity

Don't believe everything you hear.

Theories, philosophies, and subjective human experience aren't always enough for the skeptical mind. We can't depend on hunches and conjecture. Sometimes we need facts to convince us that something is true.

Holy wow creativity works, but you don't have to take my word for it. Science offers proof I'm not making this stuff up—the evidence is overwhelming. But more than that, scientific knowledge celebrates God's unmatched creativity and genius.

I won't spill too much ink explaining all the intricate details of the following scientific data. This chapter is a *very* general overview of highly complex information. If you want to clarify anything in this chapter, try looking it up online or in an encyclopedia.

### Zips and Zaps

Here's a quick biology lesson, in case you've forgotten since high school. The nervous system has billions of neurons. When we learn something, messages travel between the neurons through synapses (the gaps between neurons), and our brain remembers those connections. The more connections our brain makes, the easier it becomes to do things like ride a bike or play the piano. We can't grow more neurons, because they're the only cells that don't reproduce, but our brain can decipher an infinite number of connections between the neurons.

Neurons (aka brain cells) are complex little machines. If you could see one up close, it looks like a tiny tree. It has a bunch of branchlike things called *dendrites*. These dendrites transmit electrical impulses to each other. When cells' dendrites "talk," it's called a "dendrite connection."

Interestingly, when scientists studied Albert Einstein's brain, they found evidence of an unusually high amount of these dendrite connections. Einstein frequently credited imagination with his ability to conceive complex theories. Coincidentally, his own brain provided physical evidence that he was probably right.

dendrites

The more dendrite connections your brain makes, the easier it becomes to do things. Catalysts give your brain new connections—often random, unexpected, and unpredictable. Over time your brain is trained to make these kinds of connections more naturally, and creativity strengthens.

So neuron connections = learning. New connections = creativity.

When you were a kid, you learned not to play with fire. Your brain made various connections with fire, depending on your experience. You felt it, smelled it, watched it burn, heard about it, and saw images of its effects. All of this information sparked neural pathways in your brain that burned a lasting message: Fire is dangerous.

The creative process is no different. Our unique experiences spark new connections in our mind—often of things completely unrelated. This results in creative solutions: using a chair for a doorstop, hammering a nail with a frying pan, using a bucket for a stool. Or, like Jesus did, using a fish, a coin, or a stone to illustrate spiritual principles.

We learn by making new connections.

Try it out now with this activity.

## Don't Just Read It. Do It!
### DENDRITE DANCE
**Materials Needed:** Harmonica, piano, or other musical instrument
**Estimated Time:** Five to fifteen minutes
This exercise demonstrates how the brain learns from new neural connections.

1. Find a musical instrument you don't know how to play. A harmonica works well because learning the sounds isn't as visually clear-cut as the buttons, pedals, and strings of other instruments; however, any instrument works.

2. Without the aid of a songbook or instructor, teach yourself to play "Amazing Grace." Try to spend at least ten minutes learning the song.

As you find the right notes, your brain is making new connections and remembering those connections. After a few minutes, you'll likely have stitched together at least a recognizable line or two of the song. Your brain has routed together new neural pathways—creating connections it hadn't made before.

**3.** Consider these questions:

≋ Our brains make new connections every day. What are some things your mind has learned in the past week?

≋ Of those things you've learned recently, which things did you learn from what someone said to you? Which things did you learn from experiencing them?

≋ When we learn biblical truths, our brain connects those principles with other things we know—images, previous experiences, metaphors. What kinds of connections will help your students remember biblical truths?

## Brain Food

You're not reading this book to become an expert on nutrition or biology. But people frequently ask about whether food and supplements really have an impact on the brain and its thinking process.

You'll find as many opinions as there are experts. Scientists are nowhere near reaching a consensus on the subject. For one thing, it's a very complex issue. Thousands of variables make conclusive research difficult.

However, we do have a lot of reliable information. And the more you know, the better choices you can make about it. This section provides only a brief summary of two general points of view.

For the most part, you can select from two prevailing approaches to feeding the brain and maximizing its creative potential. Both are backed with scientific study, and both seem to work. You might consider being a purist or a pragmatist.

### The Purist

Common sense tells us we need to eat the right kinds of food to keep our bodies healthy. The brain is no exception. Creative thought needs a well-nourished brain. The purist chooses the way of maximum health.

Basically, your body will produce most of what your brain needs if you eat a balanced diet every day (especially protein and antioxidants) and drink water regularly. Most scientists agree this general philosophy is right. The purist stays committed to this and reaps the benefits of a truly healthy brain.

For a list of the right kinds of foods and how much of them you should eat, see the updated and revised food pyramid at www.usda.gov.

### The Pragmatist

Caffeine and sugar.

These are the fuels that keep the pragmatist going. The pragmatists understand that a healthy diet is the best choice. But they think it's either unrealistic or too much work. And besides, many studies show that coffee, tea, and caffeinated soda can give your brain a mental boost. Caffeine makes you less drowsy, more alert, and improves your concentration and reaction time. You can actually make fewer mistakes and think more broadly when you have caffeine in your system.

Just remember that the effects of caffeine are temporary (an hour at best). However, it's addictive, and even minor withdrawals can cause headaches and other symptoms. Moderation helps.

Some friendly advice for pragmatists—you really should avoid fatty, high-carbohydrate, greasy, buttery, fried, or heavy foods. They actually slow you down and dull your mind.

### The Right Path?

Most readers are going to stick with their current habits. But if you're genuinely interested in optimizing the health and performance of your brain—which will improve your creativity—seriously consider the following.

- Be dedicated to a balanced diet, including lighter meals and fruits and vegetables.
  - Eat plenty of complete protein in soybeans, shellfish, nuts, and whole grain cereals.
- Use caffeine in moderation.
  - Drink plenty of water.

That's how it works. This is how God created the body to function. If you commit to it, your creativity level will show it.

## Left Brain Versus Right Brain

It's actually true—each side of our brain thinks differently.

The left side of the brain processes information rationally and linearly. It keeps things in order, sets patterns, and sees in black and white. The left side is deductive and analytical, making judgments based on known facts.

LEFT BRAIN    Right brain

The right side processes the nonlinear, nonrational information (oh, what a pretty butterfly!). It's able to think abstractly (wouldn't it be neat if we could live in a giant cookie!) and doesn't rely on logic. The right side is our imagination's playground, where we conjure up art, myth, and wonder (yes, Thursday is probably round).

Most schools train us to use our left brain to interpret the world and solve problems. The right brain is usually told to be quiet and go play somewhere else.

When we think of an idea, our left brain tries to make sense out of it. How much will it cost? What are the drawbacks? Have we done this before? It makes up rules and enforces them.

But our right brain is open to new ideas. The right side dreams up the possibilities, no matter how odd or outlandish. It's capable of thinking outside of the norm and is unaware of limits and definitions.

This physiological reality helps to dispel the myth that "play" is flaky and only "serious" creative approaches are worthwhile. Those "serious" methods are fine, but they typically only use the left (rational) side of your brain. Letting our minds play with ideas requires the right side, too. You're using more of your brain that way.

For most people, one side usually dominates the other. You can test yourself by finding out which side of your body you use the most, including your eyes, arms, hands, feet, legs, smile, and thought patterns. For example, if you wink with your right eye, it's controlled by the left side of your brain. When someone asks you a question, which direction do your eyes go while you think of the answer? If they go to the left, your right brain controls that action.

No matter which side dominates, you can always learn to make more use the other side. Switch your watch from one wrist to the other. Draw pictures with your less dominant hand. Kick a ball with the opposite foot. Learn to allow your right brain the freedom to think (and dominate) during your creative sessions.

*Important note: Don't try to free your right brain by the left brain's rules.* Many approaches to using more of the right side of the brain to solve problems are still left-sided thinking. The right side is nonrational and nonlinear, so we need to use nonrational and nonlinear means of setting it loose.

Thinking in terms of the random, spontaneous, and unpredictable is a function of the right brain. It will help you be more creative, and you'll be using more of your mind's capacity.

You could say being creative is the *right* thing to do.

## Memory

We could not possibly be creative without the ability to remember.

Even the most simple acts of creativity require our memory to help us out. We couldn't draw a picture without a memory to tell us what to draw. We couldn't make a sandwich without memories to tell us what tastes good on a sandwich.

Memory is creativity's warehouse. Or, if you prefer something more imaginative, memory is creativity's treasure chest.

Scientists have found (so far) that memory appears to be the only function that's not limited to one or two regions of the brain. Memories seem to be saved and transmitted all over the brain.

Improving our memories will improve our creativity. However, many of the memory training courses you'll find train people to use association techniques to remember information. These methods only work for certain kinds of retention, and it's often short-term.

Recent science shows us that eidetic (highly vivid and detailed) memory comes from a moment of "interested intent"—being totally present in the moment with whatever you're experiencing. Being in the moment (or being "focused") improves your memory significantly.

So be present in your experiences. It's what James was referring to when he said to look "intently" at God's law (James 1:25, NIV). Paul encouraged the Colossians to "make the most of every opportunity" (Colossians 4:5). Mary was "present" with Jesus when he scolded Martha for her busyness (Luke 10:38-42).

Have "interested intent" when you're experiencing life. Let distractions fall aside. Pay attention. In other words, be the ball.

## senses

God gave us senses to help us experience the world and give us a capacity to respond to it. Your senses are tools that can open up the world in new and unexpected ways.

Contrary to what most people believe, we have more than five physical senses. Besides sight, sound, touch, smell, and taste, senses like balance, temperature, pain, and spatiality give us a greater depth of experiencing the world around us.

Being more acutely aware of all our senses can open up new connections and expand our creative capacity. Taking advantage of our full array of senses in youth ministry can also help us experience God's truth in fresh, memorable ways.

When creating holy wow experiences for your teenagers, consider how each of the senses might be affected. Ask yourself questions like, "How would this smell? What does it taste like? What happens if I touch it? Is it hot or cold? Does it hurt?"

If the sense questions don't seem to apply to your issue ("Does forgiveness smell?"), think of them in a different way: "If I could eat this topic, what would it taste like?" "If this activity had an odor, what would it smell like?" "If I could reach out and touch this idea, what kind of texture would it have?" Just by asking these metaphoric questions, you can discover a variety of original thoughts and fresh perspectives.

Here's some science-based information regarding our senses, and how we can maximize them in our creative processes.

## Color

God created color as one of nature's languages. Colors have meaning, and they speak volumes. They affect our moods, stir emotions, and help us define our world. If we understand the fundamental meaning of colors, we can use them to enhance our experiences in both creativity and ministry.

Here's a basic color lexicon you can use as a reference in your creative activities:

**Cyan** (greenish-blue)—Cold, analytical, intelligent

**Sky Blue**—Calm, true, honest

**Violet**—Deep, thoughtful, reflective

**Purple**—Royal, majestic, exciting

**Mauve**—Stylish, cultured, impressive

**Pink**—Sensitive, lovely, feminine

**Red**—Powerful, aggressive, demands attention

**Orange**—Stimulating, zesty, tangy

**Gold**—Rich, sunny, joyful

**Yellow**—Startling, anxious, sharp

**Lime**—Youthful, fresh, naive

**Green**—Mature, strong, natural

**White**—Pure, peaceful, sterile

**Black**—Elegant, mysterious, serious

Consider using specific colors when choosing catalysts for your creativity sessions. For example, if you are conceiving an experience on a subject like relationships or sexual purity, you might use catalysts made from warm, bold colors like red. Or if you're creating a lesson about choices, you might take advantage of neutral colors such as gray or light blue.

Color communicates, whether you mean it to or not.

## Light

I could give you a lengthy explanation about "narrow light spectrums" versus "full-spectrum light," but here's what you need to know: As much as possible, depend on natural light.

Fluorescent bulbs and the flicker of computer screens strain your eyes, tire you out more easily, degrade your concentration, cause you to make more mistakes, and can even make you grouchy.

Natural (full-spectrum) light is universally better. Look for bulbs that produce light that is closest to natural sunlight.

## Sound

Various kinds of music and sounds can actually slow down or speed up brain waves. Classical music and certain forms of jazz have shown a measurable ability to optimize cranial activity.

## Climate

You know all about the difference between a cold shower and a hot shower. Room temperature, although not as dramatic, also affects your senses and your ability to think.

Turn down your thermostat a little. Optimal temperatures for creative activities are typically between 66 and 70 degrees, but people's individual preferences vary greatly. Just be sure it's not too warm—you'll get drowsy.

If you can't control your climate, don't fret over it. Thomas Edison didn't have air conditioning.

### Odor

Aromatherapy is popular for a reason—it works. Soothing scents can calm the body and the mind. More vivid odors can stimulate stronger responses.

Odors can bring back a rush of highly intense memories. You know this. Find ways to use it to your advantage in your youth ministry. If a specific scent can spark a memory about a teenager's relationship with Jesus, it'll leave an indelible—and even eternal—impression.

### Taste

"Taste and see that the Lord is good" (Psalm 34:8).

The Bible makes hundreds of references to flavor, and close to half of them are figurative. God gave the tongue perhaps the most acute sensitivity of all our senses, and then used numerous food metaphors in his Word to help us understand his ways. Christ chose this sense to be the basis for a ritual he initiated—communion.

If I asked you to name your favorite foods, you could list a bunch with hardly a blink. And your mouth would probably salivate just thinking about them.

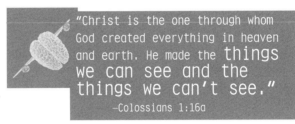

"Christ is the one through whom God created everything in heaven and earth. He made the things we can see and the things we can't see."
—Colossians 1:16a

The cravings can be almost instantaneous; it's that strong a stimulus.

The sense of taste can be a stimulating catalyst for creativity, as well as a powerful part of experiencing the truth of Scripture. The church almost corners the market on doughnuts already...let's see what else we can pull out of the cupboard.

### Case Study: Ben & Jerry's

Since we're on the subject of food, this might be a good time to point to a premier example of a team that defied conventional wisdom and used its creativity to make a mark on the world.

When Ben Cohen and Jerry Greenfield started their humble shop in a renovated Vermont gas station, they didn't envision a global empire. These were guys who loved ice cream, and they wanted to share their passion with everyone else. With a hand-cranked freezer and a bit of ingenuity, Ben and Jerry made the kind of ice cream *nobody* else was making. Chunks of chocolate chip cookie dough in ice cream? Who in their right mind would ever...

To this day, originality and creativity drive the Ben & Jerry's company. It cranks out flavors everyone else can only copy, and a copy is just a copy.

Youth ministry can learn a lot from this approach. Are you so passionate about Jesus Christ that you're able to create new ways for everyone to love him and celebrate him?

By the way, ice cream's not likely to be considered an actual "brain food" per se. But I can attest to its psychological benefits. If you need your food to *inspire* you, sometimes nothing beats a rich, creamy, chunky, chewy pint of your favorite flavor.

## Don't Just Read It. Do It!

### FLIGHT FOR LIFE

**Materials Needed:** A stack of paper, pens
**Estimated Time:** Thirty to sixty minutes
This fun exercise is designed to drive you to combine ideas using a random method. It only works with a small team.

1. Select a ministry activity you want to generate ideas for, such as a community outreach or fundraiser. Or you may select a study topic, such as loneliness or honesty.
2. Beforehand, fold about twenty paper airplanes.

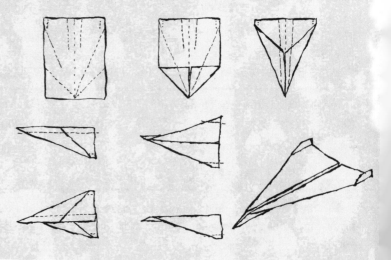

3. Sit together in an informal circle. Explain to your group the purpose of the meeting: to generate ideas for your ministry activity or topic. Give them the instructions that follow, and remind them that this is not a game or competition (but they can still have fun!).

4. Give each person a pen and a few blank paper airplanes. Have each participant write a comment on an airplane according to these L.I.F.E. directions:

❦ First, write love links. How does the concept of love fit with your activity or topic? How could love be manifested in your activity or topic?

❦ Second, write if only ideas. "If only we could do…" or "If only teenagers could understand…" and so on.

❦ Third, write firsts. What are some things or ideas your teenagers might experience for the first time through your activity or topic?

❦ Fourth, write expectations. What do you hope to get out of this activity or study? What does the result look like?

After each written comment, toss the plane to another person. Upon receiving a plane, a person should write an additional thought on the plane and then toss it to someone else. Encourage everyone to read all the ideas and comments on each plane before writing a new one.

5. Continue tossing your planes and writing comments for at least fifteen to twenty minutes. Then gather up all your planes and read them aloud together. Have one person record all the ideas on one main list. Talk about the comments and find new connections and ideas for your subject.

**Take It Deeper:** Buy a variety of "brain foods" for your group to eat before and during your activity. Choose foods such as raw fruits and vegetables, raisins, soy nuts, almonds, shrimp cocktail, shellfish, chocolate, whole-grain snack crackers, cheese, milk, coffee, tea, water, caffeinated soda, pure juice, and energy drinks.

**Connect It to Your Youth:** Give each student a pen and a couple of airplanes. Tell them a little about the topic you'll be discussing. Then have them write comments, questions, or ideas about that topic on their planes. Have them toss and circulate their planes. After fifteen minutes, have them gather all the planes and discuss their comments and questions together.

## WHISPERS AND SCREAMS

**Materials Needed:** Paper, pen

**Estimated Time:** Sixty to ninety minutes

Since we've talked about caffeine…this exercise stirs your thinking with new environmental catalysts. It also provides opportunities to consider the impact of biblical messages outside the church building.

1. Take a walk or slow drive through a busy, commercial part of town, preferably with a partner.

2. Look for any visible signs of a major soda brand—on signage, in restaurants, littered cans—anywhere and everywhere. Some will be subtle (a "whisper"), and some you can't miss (a "scream"). Mark all those places on your notepad.

3. After completing your list, stay in that bustling environment and consider the following questions:

    ♪ How many of those messages would have been invisible if you hadn't consciously been looking for them? Which ones would you have noticed?

    ♪ How might the message of Christ look in each of those instances? What would the messages say on the side of a cup, on a billboard, and so on?

    ♪ How is selling a soda brand similar to telling people about the gospel? How is it different?

    ♪ Considering your list, how might you combine content (Christ's gift of salvation) with context, to send a memorable message? In other words, what would it take to make someone stop and say, "Wow"?

**Connect It to Your Youth:** Take your teenagers on a field trip and have them do a similar exercise. Give them each a notepad and pencil and have them form groups of three. Have each group look for a different major brand. After they create their lists, bring them together and read Romans 15:20. Then ask them the same questions as above.

# Chapter 8

## 1+2=12—Relational Creativity

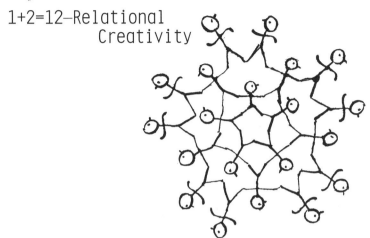

The church is people.

*People* is plural.

God created his people to work together. All throughout Scripture you find a common thread: relationships. Virtually nothing happens without the intersection of a life with another life. Every command, every virtue, every fruit, every consequence is directly connected with you and at least one other—whether it's God or your fellow sheep.

Yet too many (*way* too many) youth workers try to solve ministry problems on their own. Even if you're the only youth leader at your church, you're still not an island. You need healthy relationships to be effective. (I don't need to shout too loudly from this soapbox. Read Dave Chow's profound book *No More Lone Rangers* for an in-depth and practical manifesto on the subject.)

God says everything hangs on right relationships (Matthew 22:37-40). Creativity, too, functions best when it's shared. Putting two minds together doesn't just double your brain power. It increases the possibilities *exponentially*.

With creativity, one plus one equals so much more than two.

## You$^2$

When it comes to being creative, sometimes you just have to crank it out alone. By ourselves, and only by ourselves, we have to stretch our minds, take care of our brains, and strive to gain understanding.

Individual creativity is joyfully necessary for a number of activities, such as

- ► Painting artwork
  - ▷ Writing a novel
  - ▼ Dancing a solo recital

Sometimes individual creativity is the only option. Some examples:

- ⊙ Escaping a locked room
- ◑ Surviving alone in the wilderness
  - ◐ Rescuing an unconscious victim

The potential of "you" is virtually infinite. One person can do and create beautiful, genius, original masterpieces. Within ourselves is a wellspring we can drink from more deeply than we can imagine.

But how far can *you* go?

What if you could put yourself in a room with another "you"? Both of you would share the same experiences, same opinions, same vocabulary, same tastes, same everything. Even if you had some great ideas, they're likely to be the same ideas repeated over and over. It wouldn't matter if there were nine of you. It would amount to nothing more than a team of cloned dictators.

An apple plus another apple is still apples.

You need more than you.

## (You x She x He)$^n$

Yes, there's an "I" in SHINE. But there's also a "she" and a "he."

Alone, you can only get so far. With others, you can go infinitely farther.

When you work with another individual, you're adding that person's entire background, memories, experiences, and knowledge to the table. Your two sets of ideas are going to be different, and they're going to build on each other as you work toward a solution.

Add a couple more people, and all those brains work together to generate an even greater number of ideas. This collective creative power grows prolifically—the "wow" potential multiplies many times over.

Team creativity not only increases the *quantity* of new ideas, but it dramatically improves the *quality* of your ideas. Varying viewpoints help you evaluate and rework them to make your ideas even better.

Team creativity is also more efficient, since you can generate ideas at a much faster rate. By developing a greater number of high-quality ideas, you reap the benefits of saving time and conserving energy.

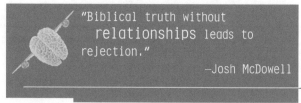

"Biblical truth without **relationships** leads to rejection."

—Josh McDowell

An apple plus flour, sugar, and cinnamon makes for a lot more fascinating combinations.

Something to think about: Team creativity does, however, reach a point of diminishing returns. Limit your small group creativity sessions to six or fewer people.

## (You x She x He)$^n$ + Holy Wow = Them$^x$

When a youth worker partners with other church leaders, parents, volunteers, and students to create holy wow, it spreads. This is an equation for contagious evangelism—fulfilling the Great Commission as effectively as we can.

Intentionally building your ministry around relationships is absolutely essential to helping students learn and apply biblical principles. Let relationships permeate everything, from your creativity to your holy wow experiences to your day-to-day practices. No relationships—no life transformation.

Creating a fresh, memorable Bible experience isn't easy. But team creativity can help you create holy wow after holy wow after holy wow. Working together makes it immeasurably more likely that you will.

# Scripture Says...

Listen up!

God's Word gives us plenty of admonishment about getting feedback from others. The Bible warns us about being dependent on ourselves. It's dangerous and slippery. If we're wise enough to get the right advice, it pays off.

Your creativity isn't any exception—it's highly personal and subjective. Talking to others can help ensure your ideas are on the right track.

Think about the following verses:

⊙ "Many advisers make victory sure" (Proverbs 11:14b, NIV).

⊙ "Plans fail for lack of counsel, but with many advisers they succeed" (Proverbs 15:22, NIV).

⊙ "Destruction is certain for those who think they are wise and consider themselves to be clever" (Isaiah 5:21).

⊙ "We work together as partners who belong to God" (1 Corinthians 3:9a).

⊙ "And don't think you know it all!" (Romans 12:16b)

Memorize these verses! Paste them on your wall! Write them down in your creativity journal!

## Small Group Dynamics

Despite the huge rewards of working with a partner or small group, the dynamics become much more complex. Small groups are minicommunities, and their character depends greatly on the individuals involved. Even if your group is only together for one hour, the nature of a small group typically stays the same.

A small group (of three to six) has some unique characteristics. You need to be aware of what happens in a healthy small group. Here are some generalities:

- *Everyone should participate.* No observers allowed. You're not doing this stuff to be watched like a fish in a tank. You may be amusing, but don't become amusement.
- *Roles differ.* Not everyone has to contribute in the same way. People with dissimilar perspectives and personalities add variety to the group, which multiplies the creativity factor. Some will be leaders, some recorders, some encouragers, some questioners, and so on. Allow this diversity to enable new ideas to be discovered.
  - *A feeling of belonging legitimizes the group.* If participants are going to contribute, they need to have a sense of camaraderie with the other members. They also need to have a sense of being a part of something larger than themselves.
- *People define themselves by their associations.* Your group is a significant part of how the members think they will be perceived by others. Make your group something they can feel confident about being a part of. Your holy wow creative sessions are all about finding new, memorable ways for teenagers to experience their relationship with Christ. That's a great cause for a group to get behind.
  - *Disagreement is inevitable.* And actually, it's healthy. Attempt to discuss subjects laterally (no one person rules, not even the leader), and try to reach consensus.
- *There's always a chatterbox.* When you've got at least four or five people involved, you'll always have one person who loves to hear himself or herself talk. That's all right, just be sure to not let that person dominate. And if it's you, be extra careful.
  - *There's always a critic.* You'll inevitably have a resident pessimist. They call themselves "realists"; that's OK, too, because they keep reality in the picture. But don't let them be too critical before you're actually evaluating your ideas.
- *There's always the quiet one.* Not a pure observer, but they like to think before they talk. Regularly ask them what they think.
  - *Power shifts.* The group, even in the short term, is a living organism that needs to act as a unit. But influence will flow back and forth, and ideas will rise and fall. Reinforce the unity of your group by regularly referring to the purpose and goals of the group.
    - *Competition creeps.* It sneaks up on even the best of us. Part of the power struggle feeds competition. In a small group, this can inhibit productivity. Don't let ideas compete. No one should try to be the "winner."
  - *No personal agendas allowed.* Don't let your or anyone else's individual agenda taint the group's purpose. Let the common goal rule while you're together.

⊳ *No group will be perfect.* You'll run into problems. At least you have the ability (usually) to invite whomever you wish to your creative sessions.

❯ *Small groups are uncomfortable.* Especially for introverts. But their benefits far outweigh the anxiety. Counter it by being inclusive, encouraging, and fun.

⊳ *Teasing is unacceptable.* It may seem like harmless fun, and everyone (including the victim) might laugh. But teasing destroys a person's confidence and crushes his or her creative spirit. Kick bullies out.

❯ *A successful, healthy group refers to "we" and "us."* The members don't even think about "I" and "me" until it comes time to serve.

## Rules

Creativity likes to buck the system.

When we work in a process that's random, spontaneous, and unpredictable, we're opening the door to a little bit of anarchy. It's one thing to let birds of chaos fly around in your own mind. But let those birds loose over a group of people trying to get some work done, and—well…

While creativity is willing to break the rules, we still need to have some kind of guidelines in order to be productive and stay on task.

It's entirely OK to agree upon a set of parameters for your creative sessions. When making your "rules," keep these suggestions in mind:

❯ *Set a goal.* First and foremost, decide what the purpose of your creative session is intended to be. At the end of your time together, you should be able to say you met your goal—or created a new one.

⊳ *Make a plan.* Never, never, never, never, never start a session by saying, "Anybody got any good ideas?" Know precisely which exercises and activities you're going to use, and be prepared with all the necessary supplies *before* the meeting starts.

❯ *Have a leader.* Someone needs to facilitate the session, encourage participation, and keep it on task. Lead by example and with a servant's heart. Don't be a dictator.

⊳ *Explain the process.* Briefly and clearly let everyone know why you're doing what you're doing. Let them know that your random, nonlinear process will be unpredictable but will lead to new ideas. Describe what a holy wow experience should achieve.

❯ *Write everything down.* Don't let note taking distract you, but make sure you can refer to your ideas at any time. Also, don't limit your notes to words—draw or clip images that represent your ideas visually.

⊳ *Listen.* Encourage everyone to pay attention to what others are saying. Ideas build off other ideas, so we need to be sensitive enough to hear them.

- ● *Stay open.* Sometimes the creative process will stray down unexpected but worthwhile paths. If your group seems to be onto something good, follow it, even if it changes your original goal.
  - ▷ *Follow directions.* If you're using one of the exercises in this book, do your best to do precisely what it says. These proven, tested activities will work if followed as written. But, of course, feel free to venture as needed!
- ● *Honor time.* We're all busy, so set a time limit and stick to it.
  - ▷ *Respect each other.* No one but Jesus is the star of the show. Everyone's opinion matters. Everyone has something to contribute. Just because someone says something that doesn't seem as valuable, don't ignore all their other contributions.
- ● *Pray.* God is with you. Include him in the conversation.
  - ▷ *SHINE.* Start with the Savior. Humble yourselves. Involve everyone. Newness rules. Experience what you're discussing.
- ● *Make a decision.* Whether or not you generate a great idea, decide on a plan of action before concluding your session.

## The Deep End

As you practice relational creativity, you're doing much more than generating new ideas. You're also strengthening friendships with your colleagues.

Solving problems together is perhaps the best way for people to bond. Crisis situations and tragedies give people—even strangers—a bond that often lasts for life. Putting your minds to work on creating fascinating ministry presents a challenging, problem-solving atmosphere that will bring you closer. You'll argue, you'll laugh, you'll get frustrated, you'll triumph, you might even cry. But you'll be doing it together, and that's the food that nourishes the healthiest friendships.

### Case Study: Picking Up Butch

Sports columnist Rick Reilly once told a story about Butch. Butch lives in Vermont with his mother and is Middlebury College's biggest sports fan. Oh, and he was born with cerebral palsy.

It's a freshman tradition at Middlebury to "pick up Butch." For more than forty years, first-year athletes have toted Butch and his wheelchair to basketball and football games at the college. They also help feed him, have taught him to read, and hold his shaky hands when the games get tense. He's become as much a part of the teams as the players themselves.

Butch says, "These kids care what happens to me. They don't have to, but they do. I don't know where I'd be without them. Probably in an institution."

Reilly notes, "But that's not the question. The question is, Where would they be without Butch?"

Middlebury isn't a Christian college. It's not a church or a youth ministry. But the athletes are demonstrating the nature of holy wow creativity in action. These freshmen, in their service to Butch, are *experiencing* the meaning of kindness, humility, and grace. And they'll never forget it.

Who's *your* Butch? What kind of impact can your youth make on others in your church or in your community? The opportunities are out there. We just need to go "pick them up."

## Don't Just Read It. Do It!

### GLAD LIBS

**Materials Needed:** A photocopy of "A Night to Remember" (p. 80), pen

**Estimated Time:** Ten to fifteen minutes

This creative exercise is no fun if you do it alone. You have to involve others! The activity demonstrates the increased effectiveness of adding people to your creative process. It works well with one other person, but even better with a small crowd. Be sure to do the follow-up questions in step 4.

1. Make a copy (or several copies) of "A Night to Remember."
2. Ask a partner or small group to give you random nouns, verbs, adjectives, and adverbs, and fill in all the blanks on the page. Make sure to keep it clean—this activity is not intended to become offensive or disrespectful.
3. Read the complete story aloud to your partner or group.
4. Discuss the following questions:
   * Some (if not all) of the sentences are likely silly or nonsense. What would be the effects if we actually did an event like the one we just read? Would it be memorable? Why or why not?
   * Describe the memories teenagers would have of this specific event. Would anything help them remember or apply biblical truths? Why or why not?
   * What could you modify in the story to make it relevant to biblical truth or our relationship with Jesus?

**Connect It to Your Youth:** Create original "glad libs" for your youth group. You can do this by writing out a short story involving your own ministry, including local people, places, and things. Then cross out a variety of nouns, verbs, and adjectives, creating blank spaces. You might also add a few adjective spaces if you haven't been too descriptive. Have students do them together in small groups, then tie the activity into a lesson about how we can change our perceptions of the world, God's Word, and our relationships through what we contribute.

# A Night to Remember

Last Friday night, our church sponsored a _____ youth
<sub>adjective</sub>

event that we'll not soon forget. When we invited the teenagers to

come, we sent them a _____ and _____
<sub>noun</sub>                <sub>adjective</sub>

_____ in the mail. Most were surprised, but a few said,
<sub>plural noun</sub>

_____ ! I'll be sure to _____ as many
<sub>interjection</sub>                    <sub>verb</sub>

_____ friends as I can." Needless to say, our ministry team
<sub>verb</sub>

was very _____ .
<sub>adjective</sub>

When the teenagers arrived that _____ evening, some
<sub>adjective</sub>

were wearing _____ on their heads, while others brought
<sub>plural noun</sub>

lots of _____ _____ . We _____ played
<sub>adjective</sub>      <sub>plural noun</sub>        <sub>adverb</sub>

an icebreaker game called "_____ _____," but one
<sub>adjective</sub>      <sub>noun</sub>

student _____ ate one of the _____ . We prayed
<sub>adverb</sub>                            <sub>plural noun</sub>

_____ , then _____ our next game, "Musical
<sub>adverb</sub>              <sub>past tense verb</sub>

_____ ." Two girls got their _____ and
<sub>plural noun</sub>                        <sub>noun</sub>

_____ mixed up, so we had to _____ as
<sub>noun</sub>                              <sub>verb</sub>

_____ as possible.
<sub>adverb</sub>

The best part was next. We set up several _____ worship
<sub>adjective</sub>

stations, where the students _____ with candles, then
<sub>past tense verb</sub>

_____ sang a song about _____ and his
<sub>adverb</sub>                        <sub>male Bible character</sub>

_____ sheep. We were all moved by the outpouring of
<sub>adjective</sub>

_____ from our _____ hearts. Then we
<sub>plural noun</sub>        <sub>adjective</sub>

_____ washed each other's _____ feet with water
<sub>adverb</sub>                          <sub>adjective</sub>

and a _____ . Tears flowed _____ .
<sub>noun</sub>                    <sub>adverb</sub>

We finished the night _____ holding hands and talking
<sub>adverb</sub>

_____ about how we could apply the _____ to our
<sub>adverb</sub>                                <sub>plural noun</sub>

_____ lives. When the parents arrived to pick the students up,
<sub>adjective</sub>

they were surprisingly _____ . It was surely a night to
<sub>adjective</sub>

remember!

## WRAP IT UP

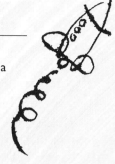

**Materials Needed:** A roll of butcher paper, a large object (such as a chair, door, television, or refrigerator), colored markers

**Estimated Time:** Preparation: twenty to thirty minutes; activity: thirty to forty-five minutes

You definitely want to involve your students in this creative exercise. You'll be tapping their minds for ideas and teaching a memorable lesson at the same time. The activity is designed for groups of students of up to about thirty; if you have more than that, consider using more than one large object.

1. Find a large object, such as a door, chair, television, refrigerator, or other item. Wrap it with butcher paper in such a way that you can still clearly identify the object after it's wrapped.

2. Using a Bible or Bible study/lesson book, take five minutes to think of several spiritual metaphors the object might represent. For example, if you choose a door, you might think of related metaphors such as salvation, hospitality, or Christ's return. Choose a main theme and write it boldly at the top of the object.

3. Direct students to write questions about the topic all over the wrapped object. Ask them to be thoughtful, honest, and tough (they will be.)

4. In private or with a partner, review the various questions the students wrote on the object. You should have a wealth of material to create a memorable lesson. Find a way to use the object as part of the students' learning experience.

**Connect It to Your Youth:**

1. First choose a topic you want to study, such as prayer, death, or grace. Then find a large object that somehow symbolizes that topic. Wrap the object in butcher paper.

2. Create one to three provocative questions about your topic, and write them boldly at the top of your wrapped object. For example, if your topic is death, and you choose a door as your object, write a question such as, "What would you do today if death were knocking at your door?" Or, "If death

were on the other side of this door, what would you see if you peeked inside?"

3. Direct students to write their answers on the wrapped object. You can have them do it during a meeting time, or you can leave it up for an extended period for them to access when they're ready.

4. Lead a discussion with your students about their answers, and tie it in to your lesson. For example, if you used a door to talk about death, you could discuss what a Christian would expect on the other side of the door versus what a non-Christian would find.

# Chapter 9

## Fill the Dumpster

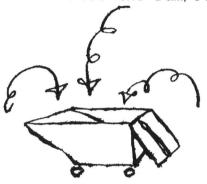

Purge everything that doesn't matter and doesn't work—specific ideas, traditions, rules, songs, games, activities, events, fundraisers, you name it. If it doesn't help grow your students' relationships with Jesus, trash it.

"Let us strip off every weight that slows us down, especially the sin that so easily hinders our progress. And let us run with endurance the race that God has set before us."
—Hebrews 12:1b

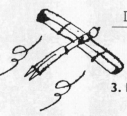

### Don't Just Read It. Do It!

1. Grab a wastebasket.
2. Clean your office.
3. Better make that ten wastebaskets.

# Chapter 10

## The Paradox Seesaw
### (or Why a Double-Edged Sword Is Better Than a Bread Knife)

How are you going to predict which ideas are going to fall like a stone and which are going to blaze trails?

You can't. You can't know if it's got enough wow or if it's an idea that won't pay off.

*That's the whole point!*

It's the very unpredictability of the outcome that makes it work. Expect the unexpected. You need to be willing to take a leap (of faith) in order to discover new ideas. Then you need to find the nerve to try them out.

But how do you know if you're being courageous—or reckless?

How could you possibly balance the "chaos" of creativity with the ultimate harmony you need in ministry?

And what if you come across as more of a knucklehead than a genius?

There's a fine line between these seeming contradictions. Creativity is full of paradoxes. There's no middle ground with  the best kind of creativity. The halfway point is moderate, neutral, and lukewarm.

So what do we do?

When given the choice between A and B, we say, "Yes!"

We learn to seesaw both sides of each creativity paradox. It's not a compromise; it's a gloriously impossible union of contrasts. It's a perpetual balancing act that, when understood and applied, makes our creativity even stronger and longer lasting.

Let's take a closer look at just how thin some of these lines are.

## The Thin Line Between Freedom and Security

We all want to be free.

We don't want to be stuck in a 6x10 prison cell for the rest of our lives. We want to be able to make our own decisions, choose our own jobs, live where we opt to live, say what we want to say, worship whom we desire to worship.

So what is *ultimate* freedom?

Being able to do whatever you want to do, right? Well, sure. Ultimate freedom means I can break loose from any kind of bondage and do it my way. No confines, no barriers, no restrictions.

"I want to run with lions across the savanna. I want to walk across the freeway at rush hour. I want to jump out of an airplane without a parachute. That's ultimate freedom, man."

We also all want to be secure.

We want to stay alive and feel safe. We want to be protected—from criminals, from accidents, from harsh weather. To survive, first we need food and water. Second, we need security.

So what is *ultimate* security?

Never, ever having to worry about anything. I can live my life completely assured that I will not be killed, maimed, or dismembered. No accidents will ever befall me. No one will ever rob me. No one can even touch me.

"I want to build my own fortress with deep bunkers and padded walls and every safety precaution known to humanity. I want to sit still and never move and be completely surrounded by my protection. Now, if you'll excuse me, I'll get back to my state of vegetation."

No one lives in these extremes—at least not for long. Somewhere in the middle is where we find a balance. Everyone decides for themselves how much freedom and how much security they want to live with.

But creativity pushes us away from the center...toward the side of freedom. More freedom means more risk, more vulnerability, more chance for getting hurt.

That's why a lot of people stay away from too much creativity. They like their security. More security means less risk, less vulnerability, less chance for getting hurt. They're less likely to experience amazing breakthroughs, but they're also much less likely to be criticized and fail. They play it safe.

Seesawing this paradox can prove challenging. Creativity forces you to test the limits of your freedom—the willingness to explore new possibilities, suggest uncharted courses of action, and do what's not been done before. Yet stretching your creativity brings you more security—it strengthens your ability to defend the truth, worship God, and identify individualized opportunities for reaching your youth.

You cannot walk this line between freedom and security. You must inexplicably choose both. Sometimes you have to jump out of the plane and free-fall. Just don't forget your parachute.

"And you will know the truth, and the truth will set you free" (John 8:32).

## The Thin Line Between Risk and Safety

We shouldn't be content to have a marginal ministry. We shouldn't accept invisibility for the message of the gospel.

But church after church after church chooses safety exclusively. I can't say that I blame them. Leaders want their churches to be a safe haven—protected from evil influences, secular culture, even each other. You bet the church ought to be a place where we feel safe.

Yet that's where most churches venture into extreme security and abandon freedom. They've become so clean they're sterile. Instead of being a safe house, some turn into a correctional facility. And many are so safe they're boring.

We want youth ministry to be safe. Safe indeed.

But let's cross the thin line and take some risks, too. Better yet, let's leap across that line, perhaps unable to see the other side, but with eyes wide open.

What exactly is a risk? It's a trigger for freedom. Suggesting a new idea, trying out a new method, and exploring a fresh approach are all risky because we don't know the outcome. We can't guarantee it will work, or predict whether it will make people go "Wow!" or "Ho-hum." (We can, however, increase our odds. I'll address that in Chapter 14.)

A risk means you really aren't totally sure how things are going to turn out. That's why church committees say "NO!" That's why youth workers don't even ask.

But venturing into creative risk can actually grow a dynamic ministry. You want kids to be fascinated with Jesus and experience holy wows. Pushing your own creative limits will reinforce the stability that makes it happen again and again.

If you never take those risks, you never discover what *could be*. Experiencing Jesus and exposing our lives to the truth of the Scriptures demands risk. Suggesting new approaches to worship or prayer or learning the Bible involves risk. Placing our whole faith in Jesus is a risk—and I can't think of a safer risk you could possibly take.

Risk is safe. Safe is risky.

## The Thin Line Between Courage and Recklessness

It takes courage to take a risk. When you're unsure of the outcome, you need to be brave or daring to go through with it.

The level of courage varies, of course. It needs to be summoned for all kinds of personal endeavors:

- Speaking in public
  - Admitting that you're wrong
- Playing a solo recital
  - Trying a new haircut
- Confronting a prodigal
  - Rescuing a child from an icy lake
- Trusting God with your money

You don't know how it's going to turn out. Overcoming the fear—however huge or small—requires courage.

So where do we draw the line and cross over into recklessness?

Something is "reckless" when it doesn't make sense to do it. You'll be safer if you don't try it. To be reckless is to be careless, even irresponsible.

The nature of courage involves a certain amount of recklessness. When Jesus cleansed the temple, it took courage. It was the right thing to do, but it came across as careless and irresponsible to many observers. Couldn't Jesus have made his point without being so violent? Surely, some would say, there was a "safer" way. Christ, it could be said, seesawed the paradox of courage and recklessness.

Youth workers, too, have a reputation among a lot of church folks of being overenthusiastic or audacious. (A lot of you like it that way.) But the last thing you want to be accused of as a youth leader is being careless, irresponsible, or reckless. That'll get you canned quicker than you can say, "Emergency room." After all, you've got the lives of teenage children in your hands.

But we're talking about *creative* recklessness, not physical danger.

Generating new ideas and trying out brand-new Bible experiences requires guts. To get to the holy wow, you've got to be brave enough to stick your neck out there.

Some people aren't going to like it. And for stupid reasons, too. "We've never done it that way." You'll get accused of being nonbiblical (which, unless it's true, is just silly). Others will say it's too hard (which is a lame excuse for being lazy), or that it can't possibly work (how do they know unless they've tried it?). They don't see you as spiritually courageous.

The existence of this resistance—on top of your own doubts—requires a courageous response. When youth workers buck the tried-and-true, they're vulnerable to the risk. When they open themselves up to holy wow creativity, they're taking a chance that it's not going to work the way they planned.

They're saying, "I'm willing to throw my security out the window."

They're embracing courage and its contradictory sidekick, recklessness.

## The Thinner Line Between Chaos and Harmony

Chaos is fun.

Admit it. Sometimes it just feels great to be a bit out of control.

And isn't faith chaotic in a way? You're not in control—you're letting God whisk you along where he wants you to go.

But, oh, chaos means trouble, too.

Just as risk is a trigger of freedom, chaos is a side effect. Freedom has the potential to set chaos loose.

When we're involved in the creative process, there's a certain amount of chaos required to make it effective. Randomness, spontaneity, and unpredictability of the process invite chaos as a guest of honor.

Yet God is not a God of disorder, confusion, and anarchy. He is the Lord of peace, unity, and fellowship. God, most truly, is the ruler of harmony.

Like the other creative paradoxes, we embrace both in the process. In the case of chaos and harmony, however, *we want harmony to win out in the end.*

No one wants a chaotic youth ministry. No one wants the truth of God to be mired in chaos. No one welcomes confusion and disorder into their church.

But, again, we're talking about creativity. In a sense, creative chaos is the road that leads to harmony. Our job is to welcome chaos, then turn it into something meaningful. We take a jumbled mess of strings, pipes, and sticks, and transform them into an orchestra.

We always come back to the goal: experiencing Jesus. As we focus on finding ways to fascinate teenagers with Christ and make the Bible memorable, chaos remains a tool in the toolbox.

Chaos is a hoot. Harmony is the wise old owl.

## The Thinnest Line Between Brilliance and Stupidity

"Stupid is as stupid does."

The thin line between creative treasures and utter nincompoopism is so thin, it would take either a fool or a genius to see it.

I know many artists who say they feel like their very creative existence straddles this thin line with each imaginative breath. Every word they write, every stroke they draw, every note they compose seems to fall on either side of the line. Will people judge it to be remarkable? or wretched? Or, worst of all, will they ignore it all together?

Of course, this is only the concern of the nonmediocre. If you choose to play safe, secure, and risk-free, you'll stay average, generic, vanilla, invisible. Holy wow wholeheartedly rejects this middle ground.

Brilliance and stupidity form a different kind of paradox. We don't embrace both. But we have to be willing to risk being one or the other. Since it tends toward extremes, it can be interpreted either way. But that's definitely a risk worth taking.

"I'll teach you how to jump on the wind's back, and then away we go," said Peter..."You just think lovely wonderful thoughts, and they lift you up in the air."

—From *Peter Pan*, by J.M. Barrie

This paradox could also be called "The Thin Line Between Success and Failure." If your idea succeeds, it'll be regarded as great. If it fails, it was just plain dumb.

Reggie Jackson hit 563 home runs (ranking eighth all-time). He also struck out 2,597 times—more than anyone else. Several studies have shown that our greatest inventors and scientists throughout history have not only blessed us with the best ideas, but also some of the biggest stinkers. What they all have in common is they were *productive*.

No one bats a thousand. No one speaks fluent genius.

No one (sanely, anyway) embraces failure and bad ideas. But to get to the fascinating ones, we have to be willing to risk creating some doozies.

To seesaw this paradox, you'll fall off a few times. Just keep climbing back on until it works.

## No Thin Lines

When it comes to Scripture, our relationship with Jesus, and the purpose of your youth ministry, there are a few lines that should be bold, broad, and never crossed.

- ▶ *There should be no thin line between confusion and understanding.* The whole goal is to help teenagers understand the Bible better, and to know Jesus better. The end result of your creative efforts and ministry ideas must be crystal clear. No guessing. No "huh?" No paradox here.
  - ▶ *There should be no thin line between the truth and relativity.* Yes, there are gray areas. Yes, we have grace and liberty. Yes, we can have stimulating discussions about doctrinal theology. But make no mistake, God's Word teaches an abundance of absolutes, and those ought to be communicated clearly, frequently, and without apology.
- ▶ *There should be no thin line between authenticity and manipulation.* You'll find no tricks involved in holy wow creativity—no scheming, no contriving, no subversion. Holy wow experiences are based in real relationship building. They're designed to help students actually learn and remember through genuine experiences. It should be as real as real gets.
- ▶ *There should be no thin line between productivity and futility.* The preacher

in Ecclesiastes may have said, "All is meaningless," but he summed it all up by saying, "Fear God and obey his commands, for this is the duty of every person. God will judge us for everything we do, including every secret thing, whether good or bad" (Ecclesiastes 12:13-14). If we're obedient and productive in our youth ministry, God will honor it. In the end you will be effective, and the results will be immeasurably eternal.

### God's Balance

Our Father assures us that, in the midst of all this chaos, freedom, insecurity, risk, and recklessness, he will help us sort through the confusion.

"And we know that God causes everything to work together for the good of those who love God and are called according to his purpose for them" (Romans 8:28).

Jesus provides us with great examples of how to thrive in these creative paradoxes. When he walked on water, he brilliantly illustrated the balance of faith between freedom and security (Matthew 14:22-33). When he fed five-thousand-plus people with a basket of food, his disciples had to embrace both courage and a bit of recklessness (Matthew 14:13-21). And when Christ was crucified, it was an unforgettable example of how necessary chaos is transformed into amazing harmony (John 19:1-30).

### Be the Story

Once upon a time everything was a bundle of contradictions. Then the people learned how to walk the tightrope. And they lived happily ever after.

### Case Study: Cornerstone

It's one of the only places you'll ever find pierced and tattooed punks alongside strait-laced preps alongside dreadlocked hippies alongside wide-eyed moms and dads—all in the name of celebrating Jesus.

Every July, the five-day Cornerstone Festival attracts one of the most diverse crowds of people on the planet. They flock in droves (nearly thirty thousand at last count) to hear hundreds of Christian bands and artists, to dance, attend seminars, and engage in art and other activities. Needless to say, it's a far (and wild) cry from the largely interchangeable, monolithic-industry-sponsored Christian music festivals elsewhere.

The event is a pure example of embracing the paradoxes of creativity. Both chaos and harmony reign here—it's free *and* secure, risky *and* safe, courageous *and* reckless, brilliant *and*—well, full of idiots. Christianity Today said it's "actually a fine balance of liberal self-expression and conservative, evangelical theology."

The festival was founded by Jesus People U.S.A., an eccentric group in their own right. For twenty-plus years they've maintained a forum for unmarketable, Jesus-loving bands; lots of amazing, well-known groups established their roots here. The founders are also committed to in-depth, intense, weeklong courses, pushing the envelope of Christian education. John Herrin, a festival director, told Christianity Today, "We believe in the Bible literally and want these same kids to be grounded biblically and live in a godly fashion."

Said one observer, "They are engaging modern culture with the gospel in ways I don't see many groups doing." In a place where the "main" stage is one of the least noticeable attractions, you know there's a lot of holy wow going on somewhere.

## Don't Just Read It. DO It!

### WHAT IF?

**Materials Needed:** Two or three magazines with a variety of photographs; scissors, paper, and pen

**Estimated Time:** Thirty to forty-five minutes

Trying to balance contradictions can be tricky. Use this creative exercise to force your thinking to embrace both sides of creative paradox. This activity is in two parts; do them in order. And be sure to consider the review questions at the end.

### Part 1

1. Page through a couple of magazines and cut out three to five photographs or images you find intriguing, remarkable, or even mysterious in some way.

2. Look at each photo one at a time, and ask only one kind of question for each photo: "What if...?" It doesn't matter what your questions are, so long as you're asking "What if?" questions. (For example, if you're looking at a snowboarder doing an incredible flip, you might ask questions such as, "What if he falls and breaks his neck? What if he tried to do that with a cup of coffee in his hand? What if his snowboard were made of glass?") Write down your questions in a column on the left side of the page. Think of at least three different "What if?" questions for each photograph.

3. In a column on the right side of the page, write down possible corresponding answers to the "What If?" questions. Think of at least two answers for each question.

### Part 2

1. Take your magazines and cut out a set of five new fascinating photographs or images.

**2.** Think of a specific youth ministry challenge you want to solve. (For example, a unique prayer activity or a discussion starter.) Write the challenge at the top of a fresh sheet of paper.

**3.** Look at each photo one at a time, and ask at least three "What If" questions for each. But this time, make your "What If?" questions relate somehow to your ministry idea. (For example, if you're looking at a photo of a snowboarder, you might ask questions such as, "What if a prayer activity were like doing a backside 360 tail-grab? What if talking to God were more like going up the lift than zooming downhill? What if we had to do a flip every time we talked to God?") The questions shouldn't be rhetorical—they should be open-ended and not necessarily have good answers.

**4.** Write down all your creative questions and answers in two columns. Look them over when you're finished and choose two or three answers that have the most potential for a youth ministry experience.

**5.** Consider the following questions:

– Rank each of the answers/experiences on a scale of 1 to 10, 1 being "ultimate security" and 10 being "ultimate freedom." How does this idea make someone feel safe? How much of a risk does this idea require?

– Rank each experience on a scale of 1 to 10, 1 being "no courage required" and 10 being "ultimate sacrifice required." How much courage does this activity require of participants? How much of the outcome is predicable?

– The process to create these ideas involved a little bit of intrigue as well as chaos—you didn't know what the photographs were going to be used for, and it initially had no logical connection to youth ministry. How much does the end result resemble harmony? How might the ideas you've generated effect a real understanding of Jesus and Scripture?

**Take It Deeper:** Instead of asking "What if?" for this exercise, substitute the phrase "If only…" for each photograph and ministry idea. (For example, if you have a photo of a snowboarder, you might say, "If only I could do a trick like that" or "If only you could snowboard in the summertime" or "If only snowboarding could be an act of prayer.") "If only…" differs from "What If?" because the answers are typically more personal and hopeful, rather than speculative.

# Chapter 11

## A Bumpy Road—
## Overcoming External Obstacles

Creativity has side effects.

People will disagree with you. They'll resent you. They'll oppose you, antagonize you, mock you, belittle you, undercut you, laugh at you, nitpick you, roll their eyes at you, point fingers at you, aggravate you, counteract you, doubt you, contradict you, rebuff you, distract you, confront you, dare you, intimidate you, accuse you, or, worst of all, ignore you.

Ouch.

It's not that your creativity is bad. It's just that new and original ideas are always—*always*—met with some kind of opposition. As you strive to make a remarkable, dramatic difference in the way your students experience Jesus and learn the Bible, it's going to make some people squirm. Even if you have a holy wow that would make angels envious, someone's not going to like it.

Does that make you a martyr? Not likely. No one should be willing to burn at the stake for creativity's sake. But you are making a stand for the cause of building relationships with Jesus and really, truly

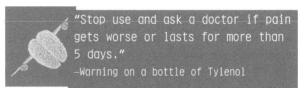

"Stop use and ask a doctor if pain gets worse or lasts for more than 5 days."
—Warning on a bottle of Tylenol

applying God's Word. Boldly and honestly venturing into that territory can get you vilified, even from well-intentioned and otherwise well-behaved church folk. How you overcome those obstacles may determine whether you ultimately succeed or fail.

As far as I know, creativity serves two fundamental functions:

- ▶ Creativity enables us to express ourselves.
- ▷ Creativity helps us solve problems.

So, because of its nature, creativity should expect obstacles to arise. In other words, if the obstacles didn't come, you wouldn't have a need to be creative. Our whole lives consist of solving one problem after another.

Obstacles aren't the antagonists of creativity; they're the very path on which it travels.

## The **Right** Response

The most important thing to remember about overcoming any kind of obstacle is to respond to it with a Christlike spirit. The SHINE mind-set applies to overcoming obstacles to your creativity just as much as it does when you're being creative.

- ▶ *Start with the Savior.* We can't forget that it's all about Jesus. No obstacle should take our eyes from that principle.
  - ▷ *Humble yourself.* Since it's all about Jesus, it can't be all about you. Philippians 2:3-4 tells us to put others before ourselves. Also, some obstacles may be there for a reason—maybe even a God-sent reason.
- ◉ *Involve others.* Our creativity gets better when we involve others, and so does our ability to solve problems. This isn't about getting people to "join your side." It's about ensuring that relationships are strengthened through the process.

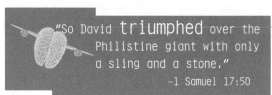

"So David triumphed over the Philistine giant with only a sling and a stone."
—1 Samuel 17:50

  - ▽ *Newness rules.* Any obstacle can be a chance for something new to happen—a new relationship to be formed, a new solution to present itself, a new life to be saved.
- ◑ *Experience it.* Embrace those obstacles and problems as an opportunity to experience the truly transforming power of creativity. Be joyful about experiencing trials because it builds our faith (1 Peter 1:6-7).

It's tempting to disregard the opinions of those who may be uncomfortable with newfangled ideas. It's easy to look down on them as not being "informed" or "enlightened." We brush them off as "old-fashioned." Let's not do that. Let's find a way to SHINE instead.

## Overcoming **Criticism**

It's the most frustrating thing about new ideas. Criticism—positive, negative, or otherwise—is a thorn in our flesh, and we don't want to hear it. You've just spent hours developing the latest and greatest, you've revised it and smoothed it out and massaged it 'til it's perfect…and then someone comes along with a hammer and messes up the whole thing.

Criticism means more work for us. Either we have to spend more time fixing parts of the solution, or we have to spend even more time reinventing it from scratch.

Worse, criticism is frequently taken personally. And, frankly, it often *is* personal, whether the critic intends it or not. Our creative ideas are an expression of ourselves, of our own individual capabilities. Creative ideas come from deep inside us—they're, in a very real sense, *part of us*.

We have three responsibilities to keep in mind for every criticism:

- *Separate the idea from the individual.* This means you. You can't control the critic's words or thoughts, but you can divide yourself from your idea.

  Don't say, "Here's what I was thinking…" or "This is my idea for the problem…" Abandon ownership of the idea, and you have the capacity to be objective about anything that's said about it.

  - *Listen.* Proverbs 15:31-32 tells us, "If you listen to constructive criticism, you will be at home among the wise. If you reject criticism, you only harm yourself; but if you listen to correction, you grow in understanding."

    Does it matter where the criticism is coming from? It shouldn't. It could be a snotty five-year-old or a detached eighty-year-old. It could be your head pastor or your younger sibling. It could be a respected leader or some Joe off the street. Smart or dumb, informed or ignorant, jerk or sweetie…at least *listen* to all of it.

- *Weigh it.* The criticism may be valid. It may be worthless. It's our responsibility to take that information and see how it applies to our situation. Don't take criticism lightly, but don't feel obligated to act on every remark, either. You carry the larger responsibility of making your ideas work, so make sure your evaluations are fair.

## Overcoming Conflict

Conflict will happen. You can't avoid it.

Whether it's in your creative process itself or in the practical execution of your ideas, you'll meet it in one form or another. Like other obstacles, conflict shouldn't be ignored or swept under the carpet. It should be faced head-on.

Conflicts can be simple and relatively painless: "I think we should use oranges for this activity." "No, I think apples would be better."

Conflicts, of course, can also be more serious: "I think we should spend this $1,000 on comfortable furniture for the students." "No, I think we need to spend the money on foreign missions."

Conflicts can get complex and nasty: "I think you're trying to prevent us from spreading the gospel." "No, I'm trying to protect our church from splitting."

Because of the provocative nature of creativity and new ideas, it's critical to handle conflict with the most positive and biblical approach possible. To manage conflict well, we must keep in mind some guidelines:

- Blessed are the flexible, for they shall not be bent out of shape.
  - Blessed are they who button up, for they shall not lose their shirt.
- Blessed are the pensive, for they shall not be written off.
    - Blessed are they who steer away from harsh emotions, for they shall not be driven up the wall.
    - Blessed are the well-rounded, for they shall not run around in circles.
        - Blessed are they who bring no baggage, for they shall not be sent packing.
    - Blessed are they who give in, for they shall not lose out.

The real beatitudes are especially helpful. Read Matthew 5:3-12. Then memorize these five basic rules of resolving conflict:

1. Listen.
2. Be clear.
3. Be tolerant.
4. Focus on the issue.
5. Stay optimistic.

Even with the most complex conflicts, observing these five simple rules, along with a genuine adoption of the Beatitudes, can keep your creativity sailing more smoothly.

### Overcoming Bias

There are about six billion people in the world.

And there are about six billion different sets of opinions about how things ought to be done.

Call it whatever you like—bias, preset agendas, prejudice, intolerance, ignorance, one-sidedness, narrow-mindedness—someone else's opinion is bound to throw an obstacle into your frolicsome jaunt down creativity lane.

> "I assure you, even if you had faith as small as a mustard seed you could say to this mountain, 'Move from here to there,' and it would move. Nothing would be impossible."
>
> —Matthew 17:20

Overcoming this obstacle isn't really any different than overcoming criticism or conflict. You have to be humble and be guided by God's Spirit.

But one thing we often overlook is our own bias.

Let me repeat that: *We overlook our own bias.*

We have our own preconceived notions about creativity, about ministry, about how to solve a specific problem. This is a particularly difficult obstacle to overcome because (1) we often don't even recognize it, and (2) if we do see it, we're forced to do battle with ourselves.

Paul faced this internal conflict too. He had been pretty full of himself. (As Paul said, "This boasting is all so foolish. But let me go on.") God popped Paul's balloon with a thorn in his flesh.

Paul begged and begged and begged God to take the thorn away. And every time, God told him, "My gracious favor is all you need. My power works best in your weakness" (2 Corinthians 12:9).

This inner, unseen bias of ours is a weakness. It's not going to go away. We must learn to accept that weakness and rely on God's grace to make it a strength.

## Overcoming Budgets

A minuscule handful of youth workers in the world have a big enough budget to do whatever they want.

Then there are the rest of us.

I can't say I have any genius solutions for making your church lots of money. You really only need to know one thing about expenses: It doesn't matter.

Creativity doesn't give a rip whether or not you have a budget. Creativity solves problems with or without cash. Holy wow creativity finds ways to help students grow in their relationship with Jesus regardless of money.

Professionals who make a living off of being creative will say the same thing. They know they have to be more inventive and find a solution that costs less. More often than not, those inexpensive approaches can be more innovative than the multimillion-dollar ones.

We all know churches are strapped for money. But God provides. If God has called you to fascinate teenagers with Jesus Christ, he's going to provide the necessary means to get it done.

## All Together Now

Sometimes the best solution for overcoming problems is right in front of us. *The rest of the church* is a hugely underused gold mine.

"Suppose the whole body were an eye—then how would you hear? Or if your whole body were just one big ear, how could you smell anything? But God made our bodies with many parts, and he has put each part just where he wants it…In fact, some of the parts that seem weakest and least impor-tant are really the most necessary" (1 Corinthians 12:17-22).

The church is a body, with lots of very usable parts. When we reach out to those other parts, we can bridge gaps and even avoid certain obstacles.

Parents, too, are often perceived as obstacles to youth ministry. Youth workers cite "lack of parental support" as the third toughest challenge they face (behind "keeping youth interested" and "competition with outside activities"). While it's true many moms and dads can be a pain in the neck, we need to understand their perspective and work *with* them. Using your holy wow creativity to find new ways of involving parents would be well worth your time.

## Finally, Grace

Obstacles? What obstacles?

"My grace is all you need."

### Case Study: Wired and Wowed

When it comes to capturing people's attention and overcoming the obstacles of a noisy, crowded culture, one pastor enlisted the help of a largely untapped resource for the church: high technology.

Ron Martoia, lead pastor at Westwinds Community Church in Jackson, Michigan, believed a traditional kind of service wasn't drawing new people into his church. He and his team concluded they needed to reach people "where they're at." So they added new layers of experience to their worship services.

Their church is not typical. Their building is a state-of-the-art facility with an auditorium wired with twenty-four hookups for real-time Internet access. They regularly project on-the-street interviews and "digital confessions" onto several screens in the sanctuary. And art is integrated into everything, highlighting the way the church embraces creativity.

But technology's only part of the story. They're making a genuine "connection" with people, no pun intended. Not only are they high-tech, they're also *high-touch.*

Westwinds sponsors periodic sensory "Encounters" at their church that are unrivaled. One example: a "wilderness" experience in which they converted their auditorium into a desert—lots of sand and cacti included. During the tactile worship experience, participants spent time at various wilderness stations, reflecting on their lives, encountering God, and otherwise being holy wowed. *Very* holy wowed.

"Awareness is crucial," says Ron of such experiences. "Each element needs to 'heighten the odds' of creating space for God to touch, heal, move, speak, blast, or do whatever he wishes."

Don't Just Read It. **Do It!**

# WORST-CASE SCENARIOS

**Materials Needed:** Paper and pen

**Estimated Time:** Twenty to forty minutes

You can never be fully prepared for every possible circumstance. This exercise is not designed to solve or even anticipate actual disasters. Instead, it helps you rehearse a *method* for how to solve them.

1. Read through one of the following scenarios, then consider the questions in step 2 for that scenario. After you've completed one scenario, read another and repeat step 2.

▶ Greg just got a call from a lawyer. He's being sued by parents whose son was sent to jail for beating up a homosexual kid at school. The son says Greg encouraged him to do it. Worse yet, the district attorney's office is considering pressing charges against Greg. Although Greg's innocent, what does he do now?

▷ Gillian's church building just burned to the ground. A wealthy and influential couple in the church offered to allow Gillian to use their spacious house for youth meetings. Gillian finds out that the couple's son was involved in starting the church fire. What does Gillian do now?

▽ A girl in Tim's youth group has disappeared. Everyone fears the worst. Two weeks after she turned up missing, Tim finds a suicide note from the girl in his office. In the note, she blames Tim for making her confused about God and says she can't live with all the doubt, questions, and judgmentalism. What does Tim do now?

▶ Jenna kicked two boys out of her youth group for refusing to stop using foul language in her meetings. The teenagers had been disruptive for months, and getting worse as time passed. Soon the pastor calls her and says the boys have "confessed" to being morally inappropriate with her. Jenna's absolutely mortified, because she's completely innocent and knows the boys are just trying to get back at her. What does Jenna do now?

**2.** Consider the following questions for each of the scenarios. Write down your answers and thoughts.

> ▶ We can't always just say no to people or a problem. But we can always provide an alternative: "No, I can't do that, but here's what I *can* do." Think of at least three alternatives.

> ▷ Consider the problem honestly from the viewpoint of every other person involved. What would you want to happen if you were in that person's shoes? What kinds of compromises would you be willing to make if you were someone else? View the problem from at least two other perspectives.

> ▽ What does the Bible say about the issues you're dealing with? List at least ten different topics that might apply to your situation, then search for at least five Scriptures that address each of those topics.

> ▶ Solving complex problems can be made easier if we substitute key elements of the situation. Change names, places, and details to add objectivity to your problem and see how it might be solved in a parallel setting.

> ⊙ Establishing integrity cannot be overestimated in protecting you in harmful situations. What can you do to build in an airtight reputation of trust and accountability with key people in your church? List at least five ideas.

> ▷ How can you turn a terrible circumstance into an opportunity to do good? For each specific problem, list at least three ideas.

## F I L M F L A M

**Materials Needed:** A small group, treats, a video or DVD, a TV and VCR/DVD player, and a comfortable setting

**Estimated Time:** Two to three hours

Overcoming obstacles often requires thinking from different perspectives. And any great story involves a protagonist working through a problem. This fun activity gives you a nonthreatening, open-ended exercise to help you develop those creative skills. You must do this with a small group, preferably with four to eight people.

1. Gather a small group of friends or colleagues together in a comfortable setting.

2. Select a movie to watch together. For best results, choose ultracheesy B movies, old sci-fi movies and westerns, or highly familiar films such as *Star Wars* and *Back to the Future*.

3. Watch the movie with the volume turned off. Everyone in the group will select at least one character to provide the dialogue for. Commit to watching the whole film in this way (refer to the TV show *Mystery Science Theater 3000* for an idea of how this can be done). Unexpected plot lines will develop, and the story will take plenty of unpredictable turns and twists along the way.

**Take It Deeper:** Use a youth ministry experience as a main part of the plotline *you* and your friends improvise. If you stick to it, you'll develop a lot of new ideas, situations, and perspectives as the movie progresses. Be sure to take notes of key observations.

# Chapter 12

## The "Un" Chapter—
## Undoing the Undone

**Multiple choice.**

Stimulating the gray matter in our skull isn't merely a matter of

_____. Viewpoints on creativity rarely see
   *(black and white, black and blue, fact)*

_____, which is why we need to get
   *(eye to eye, straight, the light of day)*

back_____. Some people think creativity is like a
            *(to basics, in black, hair)*

_____ for the mind. Others view creativity as the
   *(springboard, cardboard, carnival)*

_____ into which we dive. Either way, we should all
   *(pool, pool hall, cesspool)*

agree that creativity breaks _____. It takes us
                          *(the mold, records, out in hives)*

down _____ and opens doors to lasting
         *(new paths, town, the drain)*

_____.
   *(fellowship, battleship, dictatorship)*

When we use our creativity, it's like writing a _____
                                             *(love, resignation, chain)*

letter to God. I'll never forget the first time I painted

_____. It was _____,
*(in watercolors, the town red, myself into a corner)*     *(difficult, messy, crazy)*

but at least I did _____. The
         *(have fun, use up all the paint, not crash and burn)*

experience showed me _____ , and I
                    *(my potential, no mercy, the door)*

will re _____ it for the rest of my life. One thing's for sure—I
      *(member, gret, paint)*

no longer take talent _____.
                   *(for granted, lying down, to the cleaners)*

Know this: The result of _____ is unpredictable. We
                      *(creativity, the weather, people)*

should never assume the outcome is pre _____ . If you
(determined, shrunk, tend)

already know what's _____ you don't need creativity.
(expected, for dinner, what)

Aim for the first- _____ experience. Sometimes it's hard
(time, aid, round)

to pick _____ for good ideas. But if we work
(our brains, our noses, up hitchhikers)

_____ at it, we'll eventually find ourselves in a state of
(hard, heartily, hardly)

_____ . It can be pure _____ .
(euphoria, semi-consciousness, Alabama)                    (genius, as snow, baloney)

   Ministry's an even stickier _____. Opinions on what
   (subject, glue, sweet roll)

makes ministry _____ are more
(effective, ineffective, defective)

_____ than ever. *Holy Wow* is certainly not the
(diverse, divisive, divot-marked)

_____ word on the subject. Some points in this book
(final, misspelled, bad)

might _____ . That's
(make you shake your head, be very sharp, poke you in the eye)

_____ . You're free to decide how your ministry saves
(cool, unusual, messed up)

_____ . My hope is that nobody_____
(lives, for a rainy day, your neck)                          (throws the baby out with

_____ .
the bathwater, drowns the baby in the bathwater, takes a bath in baby water)

   However, you should consider how _____
                                    (trying new ideas, changing careers, a brain

_____ could revitalize your _____ .
transplant)                       (youth ministry, rock star fantasies, hair growth)

How might changing your _____ fascinate teenagers with
                        (approach, tires, diapers)

Jesus? What could a new _____ do to keep your
                        (experience, moon, York)

students _____ ? What might you do differently
        (captivated, in their seats, out of jail)

at _____ ? Can you make
   (youth camp, boot camp, the Camptown races)

_____ better? How
(Bible studies, up your mind, hay while the sun shines)

_____ ?
(about worship, do you do, now brown cow)

   If you're willing to jump _____ , you're taking a
                            (in, to conclusions, rope)

remarkable leap _____ . Rest assured I'll be praying for
                (of faith, year, frog)

you and thinking of you _____ . And
                        (often, whenever the phone rings, intently)

remember that ultimately the truth will _____ .
                                        (set you free, set you free, set you free)

## You Have a Choice

You can make of the holy wow concept whatever you wish. You can accept it, reject it, or just take pieces of it. Just like the multiple-choice section on the previous page, you can individualize your creativity on any level. My underlying challenge to youth workers is this:

**Push your youth ministry to be better. Don't settle for anything less than fascinating teenagers with Jesus.**

Many of you are already living up to the challenge...and then some. Thank you for your shining example. Thank you for making a difference.

Many of you are hanging in there, but you know you can do better. Thank you for persevering. Thank you for making a difference.

And many of you may be ready to move on or give up. Please reconsider. Teenagers need you. Thank you for making a difference.

No doubt there are readers who are skeptical, doubtful, or feel like they know enough already. I won't argue with that—you could very well be right. We're fellow soldiers in the battle, children of God together. But I'd like to offer a few thoughts about potential contentions, questions, and reservations you might have about the concepts presented in *Holy Wow*.

"God intends for churches to move much less predictably than most usually do. As Jesus said, 'The wind blows where it chooses...So it is with everyone who is born of the Spirit' (John 3:8). When we follow the Spirit, we become willing to innovate, re-create, reassess, step out, and risk going wherever God is."
—Michael Slaughter, *UnLearning Church*

Chapter 11 was about overcoming external obstacles. In a way, this chapter is about *internal* obstacles—our own intellectual barriers to believing something new or different.

## A Word to the Practical

Too many church leaders have adopted an unspoken ideology: "Church for the people—despite the people." Though likely unintentional, the way they operate their ministries clearly reflects this attitude. In the name of efficiency, pragmatism, and safety, thousands of churches have become a mission unto themselves—not to the people in need.

I'm really not pointing a finger so much as asking a question: Does a growing relationship with Jesus really matter? Can we honestly say that everything in our ministries contributes to helping people experience Jesus? Or are we committed to efficiency and practicality?

Breaking the norms, venturing into new territory is not "practical."

Carrying out the creative holy wow experience isn't likely to be more efficient or nicely wrapped in a package. But loving Jesus is not "practical" either—at least not from a human perspective.

## A Word to Skeptics

Skeptics have a variety of reasons to be critical.

- "I've tried that and I know it doesn't work."
- "What you're asking could never be done. It's too hard."
- "This sounds like a bunch of psychobabble to me."
- "You don't know me. You can't possibly know what I'm going through."
- "My church would never do it. You're asking the impossible."
- "I know for a fact that such and such isn't true. You're off your rocker."

I'm a skeptic myself. I'm sure I've really annoyed some people by questioning and doubting and shaking my head.

We probably agree that we shouldn't believe everything we read and hear. Proverbs 14:15-16 tells us, "Only simpletons believe everything they are told! The prudent carefully consider their steps. The wise are cautious and avoid danger; fools plunge ahead with great confidence." The Bereans in Acts 17 listened carefully to Paul's teachings, then they "searched the Scriptures day after day to see if they were really teaching the truth" (Acts 17:11).

This book is not intended to be authoritarian or universal—it's flexible by nature. No single method is going to cover all your highly individual problems.

*Your youth ministry is unique and has individual needs.* Holy Wow *gives you the opportunity to customize creative ideas to meet your own needs.*

"It's kind of fun to do the impossible."
—Walt Disney

We can agree to disagree about a long list of things, creativity methods included. However, I believe we should all be accountable for having ministry that's truly effective and purposeful.

At the least, let's find common ground in Paul's words in 1 Corinthians 10:23-24: "You say, 'I am allowed to do anything'—but not everything is helpful. You say, 'I am not allowed to do anything'—but not everything is beneficial. Don't think only of your own good. Think of other Christians and what is best for them."

## What I'm Not Saying

- *I'm not saying holy wow creativity is the only method that works.* The church had been quite successful long before I came along, thank you very much. You can use a variety of approaches to lead people to God, nurture their relationships with Jesus, and deepen their understanding of Scripture. However, I firmly believe that many of those older or traditional methods have lost their effectiveness and should be abandoned. Fresh, relevant methods are not only appropriate, but necessary. The whole point of holy wow creativity is to provide customized, individualized experiences...so a church can create its own unique experiences that immediately and profoundly grow teenagers' relationship with Jesus and help them better understand the Bible in order to apply it to their lives. Proverbs 15:2 backs this up: "The wise person makes learning a joy."

‣ *I'm not saying the church needs to change with the culture.* Quite to the contrary, we need to provide alternatives to secular, worldly culture. The church needs to stay attuned to the needs, beliefs, and trends of society so it can counter them appropriately. That doesn't mean we do the *opposite* of culture; we need to provide fascinating, Bible-based *alternatives* to culture. There's a big difference.

> ‣ *I'm not saying abandon tradition.* I love traditions. They ensure that our beliefs and our history are passed on to future generations. But let's not forget the infinite value of new experiences. They're life-changing because they're memorable. This isn't a one-or-the-other kind of thing—we can have both.

‣ *I'm not saying Bible education isn't important.* No doubt, statistics reveal disturbing evidence of this younger generation's lack of biblical understanding. They're not learning the Bible. They're not remembering its principles nor are they applying them to their lives. Sadly, most don't even know what they believe, much less why they believe it.

Is it because they're not getting enough "serious," academic teaching of Bible facts? Or is it because the *way* we've been teaching the Bible isn't working? We have to consider the possibility that the *best* ways to help teenagers remember biblical principles may be different from what we know as "serious" Bible learning. We need to be open to effective methods that make Bible lessons truly memorable. What's better: A thorough head knowledge of biblical history, numbers, and facts? or regular experiences that give us the chance to live out our friendship with Christ? Do we care more if a teenager memorizes the names, dates, and details of Israel's captivity in Babylon, or if a teenager remembers and applies the *principles* of Israel's experience? Hearing God's Word is a part of it; actually living out his Word is an intrinsically more important part.

‣ *I'm not saying you have to be outrageous.* Being over the top is not necessary for real creativity. In fact, hyperbole can be downright obnoxious and distracting. Doing the outrageous is fine so long as it's purposeful. The substance comes from the content, not from the package it's contained in.

⦿ *I'm not saying you have to turn teenagers' practical daily lives upside down.* The primary things teenagers want to accomplish in their lives don't change quickly or easily. You can't realistically expect teenagers to do something that's not a priority in their lives. To be successful, you need to look for ideas that help teenagers better achieve what they are already trying to do.

⦿ *I'm not saying creativity rules.* That's idolatry. I'm a big fan of creativity, but I recognize it as a means to an end. What better way to take advantage of this gift than to use it for God's service?

## A Word to the Tentative

You may be hesitant to try some of the exercises in this book. You have your reasons. If I could guess, I'd say any uncertainty might have to do with a discomfort with the unknown. "What might happen?" "What if I look like a fool?" "What if I try it and I get no holy wows?"

Perhaps this book doesn't need to boost your creativity so much as it needs to boost your confidence. I'm convinced this stuff works—I've used these basic concepts for years. All I can say is, "Try it out!"

You can take one step at a time—but at least take a step. The activities in this book have a beginning and an ending. They all have a goal and a means to reach that goal. Plus there is a wide variety of activities to choose from, especially if some are just too "out there" for your tastes.

The objective of this book is to make your job as a youth worker more fulfilling, more enjoyable, more effective, and ultimately easier.

I never tried strawberries until I was about sixteen years old. I was just too picky as a kid. Once I realized how delicious strawberries were, I immediately started trying other "new" foods. A whole world opened up to me, much to my mouth's delight.

The cliché here is true: You never know until you try.

## A Word to the Cookie Cutters

"I want to be a clone!"

Steve Taylor's jubilantly sarcastic anthem still rings true twenty years later. It's not about individuality. It's about being genuine and real and taking a stand for the right thing.

The title of this book could very well have been *How Not to Be a Clone in Youth Ministry.* The cookie-cutter approach may have its merits, but there's strong evidence to suggest it doesn't work in today's culture. Cookie-cutter Bible studies, events, and activities turn teenagers off. Finding a holy wow that breaks through all the conformity clutter and makes Jesus fascinating…that's anti-clone.

Doing ministry the same way over and over isn't just cookie cutting, it's bricklaying. Bricks make walls.

Most people would never admit to being cookie cutters. It's an insult. But have they considered whether their ministry operates with a "herd mentality"? Do they realize that a homogeneous approach to spreading the gospel is cookie cutting?

Excessive conformity is, in part, the result of trying to be "culturally appropriate." And, after all, what church wouldn't want to be described as "culturally appropriate"? To be otherwise would categorize you as dysfunctional or even rebellious.

Let's shift our thinking. Yes, we need to be culturally appropriate (that's the good kind of conformity). But we also need to be willing to be "functionally inappropriate." This changes the rules about how we *operate*—how we go about conducting our ministry. It's not always clean, neat, and nicely dressed. It allows you to break norms. It lets you escape the status quo. It kicks you out of Cloneville.

This doesn't suggest disobedience or disrespect. We're talking about how we function—functioning in a way that would seem inexpedient, impractical, and counterintuitive to others, but in a way that *actually works*.

When it comes to sharing the gospel, to fit in is to fail.

## A Word to the Wise

"You must unlearn what you have learned." (Yoda again.)

The Bible says it even better:

"Let God transform you into a new person by changing the way you think" (Romans 12:2).

All of us forget that the world and its "dirty devices" has diminished the child inside each of us. The world tricks us into growing up, being practical, doubting everything, becoming distracted. Shame on the world? Or shame on us? Let's shed that so-called knowledge and *unlearn*. Let's rediscover the childlike attitude Jesus talked about that—the innocent, untamed belief that anything is possible.

### Case Study: Mosaic

Thankfully, the church has cutting-edge leaders who are already proving the truth of the holy wow concept. One of the best is Erwin McManus and his team at Mosaic Church in Los Angeles, California. The leaders at Mosaic believe "the church isn't here to meet our needs. We are the church, and we are here to meet the needs of the world."

They back up that philosophy by capturing people's attention where they already are. When Mosaic wanted to have a stronger outreach to Hispanic men, they started a soccer team. When the city's soccer schedule dipped into Sunday mornings, Mosaic changed their Sunday worship schedule to accommodate it.

Mosaic does the same for its youth. The arts are very important to a lot of teenagers in Southern California. Whether it's musical, performance, written, or visual arts, Mosaic provides outlets for students to express themselves—all within the context of Christ-centered growth. In Mosaic's youth ministry, teenagers are free to dance, paint, sing, act, and write lyrics; in other words, students grow closer to God by doing things they can relate to. Of course, what churched teenagers consider art in Los Angeles may not fly in Tulsa, but Mosaic is reaching teenagers in Los Angeles, not Tulsa.

The leaders at Mosaic understand how to avoid being invisible, even in a crowded, noisy city full of attractions and distractions. It's because they make Jesus genuinely fascinating to teenagers through means they can relate to.

You can find out more at www.mosaic.org.

Don't Just Read It. Do It!

## RULES FOR FOOLS

**Materials Needed:** Paper, pen

**Estimated Time:** Twenty-five to forty-five minutes

Undoubtedly people will say, "You can't do that!"

But a lot of what you don't do has no good reason for not being done (unless, of course, it's just plain wrong). Almost everything you don't do is the result of fear, inertia, or no one asking, "Why not?"

This exercise will reverse that thinking. Do this activity with a small group.

1. Think of a specific ministry experience, such as worship through music or a short-term mission trip.
2. As a group, read 1 Corinthians 1:21-29.
3. Take ten minutes and think of all the normal "rules" for conducting the ministry experience. Some of the rules may be obvious, but challenge yourself to think of more obscure rules, as well as "assumed" rules that we usually take for granted. For example, rules for a skit might include things like "requires a script," "must only use teenagers who choose to volunteer," or "must be dramatic or funny." Push your group to think of possible rules for a full ten minutes. Write them all down.
4. Review your list of rules together. On a separate sheet of paper, write how you can break each one of those rules. Try to think of at least two or three ways you can break every rule. Some of those rules may be unbreakable, such as "must

"Man, I wish I was an adult so I could break the rules!"
—Bart Simpson

glorify God." Don't skip those rules—instead, write alternatives to those rules.

5. Review your list of rule breakers. Discuss the following:

▶ In what ways does this list challenge convention or the status quo?

▷ How would breaking some of these rules lead to a more memorable experience?

▼ How would breaking some of these rules open our eyes to a better way to grow our relationship with Christ?

▶ How would breaking some of these rules free us to use more effective ways to learn biblical principles?

## Boost Your Creativity NOW
### YOU'RE FULL OF BLOG

**Materials Needed:** A computer with Internet access

**Estimated Time:** However long you choose

Here's a fun, creative (and free) way to sound off about your passions and peeves, as well as a way to initiate meaningful dialogue with teenagers where they are—online.

1. Create your own blog (Web log) by signing up with one of several blog site sponsors. (I won't officially endorse any specific site, but you can find one through a search engine.)

2. On a regular basis (daily, weekly, or whatever you have time for), take a few minutes to write your thoughts about anything you believe might be relevant to students' lives—Scriptures that spoke to you, experiences you've had, movies you've seen, songs you've heard, books you've read, Web sites you've visited. Choose anything that's relevant.

3. Be sure to let your students know it's there. And be sure to keep it updated. They'll be paying attention.

# Chapter 13

## The Plan—
## Become an Expert in Seven Days

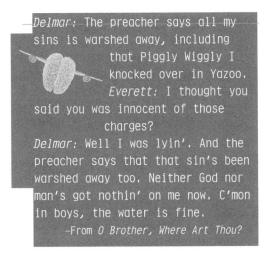

*Delmar:* The preacher says all my sins is warshed away, including that Piggly Wiggly I knocked over in Yazoo.
*Everett:* I thought you said you was innocent of those charges?
*Delmar:* Well I was lyin'. And the preacher says that that sin's been warshed away too. Neither God nor man's got nothin' on me now. C'mon in boys, the water is fine.
—From *O Brother, Where Art Thou?*

The water is fine, indeed.

But where to jump in first? If you've been "doing" this book as you've been reading it, then this chapter will just be practice. If you feel like there's too much information to soak in and you're not sure exactly where to start, then this chapter makes a great step 1.

I've tried to make experiencing the book as easy as possible. By spending about an hour a day for seven days (they don't have to be consecutive days), you can apply the major principles of holy wow creativity. And since you're already committed to dynamic youth ministry, hopefully these activities will give you a boost.

The next few pages give you a simple, organized way to apply key parts of this book step by step. Most of the instructions in this plan are meant to be done alone—for your own personal growth and for applying this book.

"The Plan: Phase 1" gives you a seven-day outline of readings and exercises that review the key elements of the holy wow concept. Each day builds successively on the previous day, so that by the end of the week you'll be applying all the principles together.

"The Plan: Phase 2" is a bonus plan for boosting your personal creativity and suggests fun, enjoyable activities you can do over another seven-day period.

## Day 1—Fascinating Teenagers With Jesus

1. Read the following Scriptures and answer the questions:
   ► Luke 10:38-42. Have you chosen the one thing in your youth ministry?

   ● Acts 2:44-47. How does your ministry compare to the early church?

   ⊙ Galatians 6:7-10. What are you sowing in your youth ministry?

   ⊙ Ephesians 5:15-17. How are you making the most of ministry experiences?

   ● Colossians 1:28-29; 2:2-10. How are you helping your students mature in their relationship with Christ?

   ► James 2:13-17. How are you helping students practice their faith?

2. Review the "How Are You Doing?" quiz in Chapter 1 (page 14). How are you doing? Summarize your thoughts here:

3. Do the "Diffendoofer Church" exercise in Chapter 1 (page 16).

**Creative Challenge for the Day:** Talk with at least one teenager about how to break through the noise of culture and get teenagers' attention. Listen closely to what they say, as well as what they don't say.

## Day 2—The "New" Creativity

1. Proverbs 18:15 says, "Intelligent people are always open to new ideas. In fact, they look for them."
   ▶ How open are you to new ideas?

   ▷ Think about the last great idea you had. How did it come to you?

   ▼ When was the last time you tried out a new idea?

2. Read the following Proverbs: 13:16, 13:19, 14:8, 16:3, 19:2, and 19:20.
   ● How does each of these verses apply to creativity in youth ministry?

3. Ecclesiastes 12:10 says, "Indeed, the Teacher taught the plain truth, and he did so in an interesting way."
   ● How are you teaching the truth in an interesting way?

4. Nonlinear creativity includes randomness, spontaneity, and unpre-dictability. The majority of creative exercises in this book involve at least one of these elements.

   Do the "Infinite Alphabet" exercise in Chapter 2 (page 25).

   ▼ Did you think of any good ideas while doing this activity? If not, do you think it would be possible if you tried it again or adjusted the exercise to fit your specific needs?

**Challenge for the Day:** Find at least one thing in your youth ministry that's typically done through a formula. Think of a new way to do that experience.

## Day 3—Time to SHINE

1. Start with the Savior—read 2 Corinthians 5:13-15.
   ▶ List all the things your youth ministry does to focus on Christ.

2. Humble yourself—read Philippians 2:3-4.
   ▶ Do all your creativity and ministry efforts lift up others instead of you? Explain.

3. Involve others—read Romans 12:5.
   ⊙ How much do you depend on yourself to create exciting ministry ideas?

4. Newness rules—read Ephesians 4:22-24.
   ▼ What could you add to your youth ministry that's new?

5. Experience it—read Ecclesiastes 12:11.
   ▼ How are you spurring your students to action?

6. Do the "SHINE Out Loud" exercise in Chapter 3 (page 34).
   ⊙ How do you think of spiritual experiences in different ways?

**Challenge for the Day:** Experience something new; something you've never done before.

## Day 4—Creative Catalysts

**1.** Read the section in Chapter 4 titled "Catalysts." Then read Ecclesiastes 10:10.

▶ What kind of catalysts can "sharpen your blade"?

**2.** Do the "Buckets" exercise in Chapter 4 (page 43).

◑ List at least three ideas or thoughts you generated from this activity.

**Challenge for the Day:** Identify at least fifty things in your office or home that could be used as catalysts to spark your creativity. Add one new one.

## Day 5—The Spirit Moves

**1.** Read Exodus 31:1-5.

⊙ Why do you think God chose an artist to be the first to fill with his Spirit?

**2.** Read Romans 8:9.

◓ How much of your ministry is controlled by the Spirit? What are one or two daily steps you could take to make a greater effort in submitting to the Spirit's leading?

**3.** Read the "Labyrinth" case study in Chapter 5 (page 50).

⊙ Why do you think more churches don't put on experiences like this?

**4.** Do the "God Encounter" exercise in Chapter 5 (page 51).

**Challenge for the Day:** Take one act of faith in your daily life—a prayer, for example—and do it in a way you've never done before.

## Day 6—Hatching Eggs

1. Read the first section of Chapter 6 about the story of *Horton Hatches the Egg*.

   ▶ How well do you exhibit stick-to-itiveness in your youth ministry? in your personal life?

2. Hebrews 12:12-13 says, "So take a new grip with your tired hands and stand firm on your shaky legs. Mark out a straight path for your feet. Then those who follow you, though they are weak and lame, will not stumble and fall but will become strong."

   ▶ How does your personal discipline affect the teenagers you are leading?

3. Read the "Pop Tarts" quote on page 57.

   ⊙ Complete the following phrase at least five different ways: "Imagine how cool youth ministry would be if the youth leader was the sort of person who _____.

   _____.

   _____.

   _____.

   _____.

4. Do the "RUTS" exercise in Chapter 6 (page 60).

   ⊙ List at least three ruts you considered changing in your ministry.

**Challenge for the Day:** Talk with your pastor, colleague, a friend, or your spouse about ways to differentiate between self-discipline and busyness.

## Day 7—Cleanse and Rest

**1.** The seventh day is a day of rest. Take a moment to contemplate all the activities you've done over the past six days.

● How have your creative abilities changed over the past few days?

● Are you challenged to try more ideas? Why or why not?

**2.** Read Hebrews 12:1.

⊙ What in your ministry to you need to cast aside?

**3.** Today you're resting from challenging creative exercises, but not entirely resting. Purge your "creative space"—the place where you've done most of the activities over the week. Discard anything that doesn't assist you in your efforts to help students grow in their relationship with Jesus.

**Challenge for the Day:** Treat yourself to a flavor of tea, coffee, or juice that you've never tried before.

## The Plan: Phase 2

### Turn Your Office or Youth Room Into a Creative Gallery in Seven Days

Here's a chance to develop your creative skills, have some fun, enjoy God's good gifts, and grow as an individual!

This easy seven-day plan is designed to boost your personal creativity, as well as provide some new, original elements to your workspace. They each require a different set of skills. Don't worry about your level of talent—the purpose of this plan is to express yourself and experience forms of art that most people don't take the time to play with.

Note: This plan is intended to be done separately from and on different days than "The Plan: Phase 1."

Spend at least one hour per day with each suggested activity.

### Day 1

Paint a self-portrait. Use watercolor, acrylic, oil, finger paints, or other paint media. You might consider using it for an object lesson about identity.

### Day 2

Write a new worship song. Use Psalms or other unexpected catalysts to inspire your theme. Teach it to your youth group and have your students create new verses to the song.

### Day 3

Draw a creative, detailed map. Use colored pens or pencils to create your own unique version of your local community, highlighting special features and local hangouts. Use it in discussions about where your youth group can touch the community.

### Day 4

Write a poem about freedom. You might get ideas from your most recent experiences with your teenagers. You can use it as a springboard for discussions about our freedom in Christ.

### Day 5

Sculpt a model of your church. It could be a lifelike representation or a "dream" church that displays everything you ever hoped for. (Use sculpting clay or, if you prefer, cardboard and glue.)

### Day 6

Photograph spiritual metaphors. Find objects that represent biblical concepts. Take inventive, unique, black-and-white pictures of those objects.

### Day 7

Rest and watch clouds. Write a list of all the things you see and imagine. Looking for shapes in clouds for just twenty minutes strengthens your creative ability.

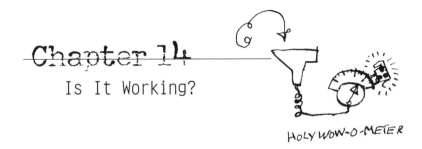

# Chapter 14
## Is It Working?

HOLY WOW-O-METER

Sorry, there's no magical holy-wow-o-meter.

You can't guarantee success with every idea; it's just not going to happen, no way, no how. Some ideas will stink. But many *will* be holy wows. And you can increase your odds of effectiveness significantly if you know what to look for.

The evaluation tools in this chapter are designed to help you identify the strengths and weaknesses of the ministry ideas you develop. The first tool is a preflight checklist that helps you think of elements you might have missed. The second tool is a post-flight evaluation that identifies how well your ideas performed.

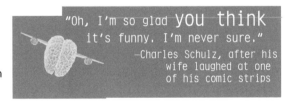

"Oh, I'm so glad you think it's funny. I'm never sure."
—Charles Schulz, after his wife laughed at one of his comic strips

Both are subjective measuring sticks that point out both positive and negative aspects. How you adjust those aspects is up to you.

### Setting the Standard

Consider the words of Paul from 1 Corinthians 3:11-13: "For no one can lay any other foundation than the one we already have—Jesus Christ. Now anyone who builds on that foundation may use gold, silver, jewels, wood, hay, or straw. But there is going to come a time of testing at the judgment day to see what kind of work each builder has done. Everyone's work will be put through the fire to see whether or not it keeps its value."

We are the builders and our work will be judged. How certain are you that your work is made of gold, silver, and jewels? The first sign: the things that will survive the fire are those that prove Jesus was truly a part of what you did. Second Corinthians 13:5 explains: "Examine yourselves to see whether you are in the faith; test yourselves. Do you not realize that Christ Jesus is in you—unless, of course you fail the test?" (NIV). Is there evidence? Can you demonstrate how Christ is among you?

The second sign to know if you're working with "fireproof" materials: evidence of spiritual fruit. When the Holy Spirit controls our lives, this fruit will be produced in us: "love, joy, peace, patience, kindness, goodness, faithfulness, gentleness, and self-control" (Galatians 5:22-23a). Are you really seeing fruit produced in the lives of your students?

## Why Evaluate?

The bottom line: We're accountable.

The Bible tells us our work will be judged. But the spiritual benefits go far beyond accountability.

We should welcome evaluating and testing because it makes us better. "So be truly glad! There is wonderful joy ahead, even though it is necessary for you to endure many trials for a while. These trials are only to test your faith, to show that it is strong and pure. It is being tested as fire tests and purifies gold—and your faith is far more precious to God than mere gold. So if your faith remains strong after being tried by fiery trials, it will bring you much praise and glory and honor on the day when Jesus Christ is revealed to the whole world" (1 Peter 1:6-7).

"Some settling of contents may have occurred during shipment and handling."
—Kellogg's Corn Flakes

Proverbs 10:17 also gives us a promise and a warning: "People who accept correction are on the pathway to life, but those who ignore it will lead others astray." If we're willing to hold our ministry ideas and ideals up to the fire, it will most definitely pay off in the end.

Why evaluate? We have great accountability and responsibility for everything we do in our ministries. Evaluating their effectiveness—beforehand and afterwards—keeps us informed and aware of how we're really doing.

## How to Identify a Holy Wow Experience

You developed a great idea, pretested it, and carried out the experience with your youth group. How do you know if it was a holy wow experience?

First of all, the most fundamental question is whether or not it helped your teenagers grow in their relationship with Jesus. Second, did it cause them to learn a biblical principle in a way they'll remember and apply?

Any good idea can sound good on paper. But once you've created some kind of clarity out of the chaos, it needs to reveal a workable function and a process that moves your students from point A to point B—from their current state of mind to a new way of thinking.

As you develop your ideas, keep in mind the three stages of the holy wow experience:

1. *The Pull:* It attracts you and draws you in.
2. *The Plunge:* It engages you. You forget about time while you're involved in it.
3. *The Push:* It makes you want to share it with others and do it again.

Just one or two steps are not enough; each experience needs to go through all three phases in the process. When all three happen, you can be confident it was a holy wow.

"Be sure to do what you should, for then you will enjoy the personal satisfaction of having done your work well, and you won't need to compare yourself to anyone else" (Galatians 6:4).

### Case Study: Chill

Chris Hill is a twenty-year youth ministry survivor and thriver. Having spent most of his career with T.D. Jakes at The Potter's House in Dallas, Texas, Chris knows a thing or two about how well youth ministry is working.

He didn't get through all those years by shying away from self-evaluation. In fact, he calls himself a "cold-blooded pragmatist." Chris recommends some key elements in evaluating the success of a youth ministry:

- Numerical growth matters. Although Chris believes this is "completely wrongheaded," he says that's how people perceive success. We've got to live in the real world, and the real world "counts."

- Spiritual growth matters. But since it's "invisible," Chris says, we need to resist the temptation of judging the fruit too harshly.

- Fitting in matters. Fitting in with your church organization, that is. Whatever your church's vision may be, you need to find some way of matching its strengths.

Chris admits Jesus would have failed by these standards. But his pragmatic side reminds him, "And they fired Jesus, too."

## Don't Just Read It. Do It!

## WILL IT WORK?
## PREFLIGHT CHECKLIST

You can't predict for sure whether your idea will fly or flunk, but this checklist will help you evaluate it beforehand so you can (1) improve your odds of success, and (2) avoid potential pitfalls. Make a copy of this page for each idea you're testing, and keep it handy for notes and reference.

### Essential Factors

For each of the following factors, don't just check yes or no; write a brief reason why it does or doesn't meet that standard.

State a clear purpose and goal for this idea. Write it in one sentence.

Does this idea clearly grow teenagers' relationship with Jesus?
O yes O no

Is it based on Scripture? List reference(s).
O yes O no

Does it make one point students will understand? Write the point.
O yes O no

Will students learn the Bible in a memorable way?
O yes O no

Is this idea experiential? Will your students *do* something?
O yes O no

Will students build their relationships during the experience?
O yes O no

Will students apply the Bible point during the experience or soon after?
O yes O no

Does this idea have a fascination factor? What is it?
O yes O no

### Have You Covered the Details?

Who should be involved? Name names.

Who shouldn't be involved?

Where will you do this experience? Are there other options?

Where will they apply it afterward?

How long will it take?

What if you run out of time?

When will you follow up?

What are the supplies you need?

When will you take notes (as you lead it, or immediately after)?

Would it help to take photographs or videotape the experience?
○ yes ○ no

**Other Considerations**
Your idea doesn't have to include any of the following, but this checklist might provide additional elements than can strengthen your idea.

Does this idea enable teenagers to grow by themselves?
○ yes ○ no

How does this idea reach detached, uninterested teenagers?

How does it give opportunities for spiritually mature teenagers to help others?

How will this idea help teenagers do more easily and effectively what they're already trying to do?

How does this idea intersect God's Word with teenagers' everyday lives?

What can you eliminate to make it simpler?

Don't Just Read It. Do It!

## DID IT WORK?
## POST-FLIGHT EVALUATION

How did it go? If you took notes during or immediately after the experience, review them. Don't simply answer "yes" or "no"—write a brief explanation.

Did you achieve your original goal? Why or why not?
○ yes ○ no

How well did the students understand the instructions?

Were the students "engaged" during the activity? (Did they seem to "forget time" as they experienced it?) Why or why not?
○ yes ○ no

How did the students connect the experience with their relationship with Jesus?

Did the experience go the way you expected it to? Identify specific elements that didn't work.
○ yes ○ no

What surprised you? What surprised the students?

Was there a single, most exciting moment? If so, what? Was there a single, most frustrating moment? If so, what?
○ yes ○ no

**OK**
to copy

Did the students ask any relevant, content-related questions? What were they?
○ yes ○ no


Did at least one student have a holy wow reaction to the experience? Who reacted, and what was the reaction?
○ yes ○ no

## Making Improvements

What could you eliminate from the experience to make it better?


What could you add to the experience to make it better?


How could you have involved different senses?


How would changing the location affect the outcome?


How might adding food or drink to this activity affect the experience?


What might happen if you involved the teenagers' parents?


What might happen if the experience were in a larger group? a smaller group? one on one?


Would the experience be more effective if you changed the application or follow-through approach?
○ yes ○ no

# Chapter 15

## How to Make Your Own Holy Wow Experiences

Time to walk the talk.

Hopefully you've been experiencing the application and practice exercises found throughout the book. Each one was specifically designed to help you better understand the principles in *Holy Wow* and give you a chance to practice your skills.

"Create wonderful things, be good, have fun."

—Klutz® Books mission statement

This chapter offers a list of fifteen different activities to help boost your creativity and develop holy wow experiences. These exercises are tools to help you develop your own unique, individualized youth ministry solutions.

The "Holy Wow Mix-N-Match" chart lists all fifteen creative exercises along with fifteen potential ministry areas. You can use any exercise with any ministry challenge. Some exercises will work better with certain ministry areas, but feel free to experiment.

Have fun with them! These tools should be enjoyable. At the very least, they're an effective alternative to traditional brain-squeezing. At the most, they'll help you create holy wow after holy wow after holy wow.

### First, a Word From Our Sponsors

Before we dive into the exercises, let's take a moment to think about (and *rethink*) how we define some of the most common ministry functions.

▶ *Reinventing Bible Lessons.* Rather than concentrate on what the teacher is teaching, how about focusing on how much the learners are learning? Are they going to remember what you've taught? Are they going to apply it? Every lesson should be memorable. Otherwise, why do it?

> ⊙ *Devotions That Rumble.* Devotions are acts of devotion to God. This is no trifle. The concept of devotion is huge. We're committing, dedicating, consecrating ourselves to God—and nothing could be less trivial. Does every devotion need to rock the world? Of course not. Does every act of devotion need to stir us and help us remember the depth of our commitment to God? I think so. Think about what a devotion *could* be…

⊙ *Alt Worship.* Alternative worship experiences give us a chance to praise, adore, and express our love to God. They can be done through song and prayer, but they can also be done creatively through art, performance, and other ways. Perhaps the only guideline we need for worship is that it be worshipful.

> ⊙ *Games With a Purpose.* Games are a fact of life in most popular youth groups. They offer fun, build social skills, and break the ice. But if our purpose is to help students grow in their relationship with Jesus, why not create games that specifically work toward that? Meaningful games can be a powerful tool.

⊙ *Writing a Skit That's Not Lame.* It's agonizing to watch students perform a stilted, poorly written script. It's not easily done, but here are a few tips: Read and reread your dialogue out loud; make sure the language is real and not forced; and go for the unexpected. That's what the creative exercises are for—to help you make your story more intriguing.

> ⊙ *Outreach That Reaches In.* Pulling teenagers *into* your ministry is certainly a challenge. Going out to where they are is altogether different. Does youth ministry have to be based in a church building? What if you took your meetings off-site, wherever teenagers are likely to be? In order to reach out like that, we first need to reach in and dig out the ideas that will work.

> ⊙ *Rethinking Short-term Missions.* The short-term mission trip provides one of teenagers' most memorable spiritual experiences. They serve under less-than-ideal circumstances and grow in character. But why just once a year? If short-term mission trips are so powerful, why not do them more often? Surely you're not letting silly things like money and time hold you back. I guarantee you can find some amazing, creative answers to these issues.

▶ *Prayer That Moves.* We get to talk with God—how cool is that? Most people agree you don't have to be on your knees…you don't have to close your eyes…you don't have to recite certain rote words. But what other things do we assume about prayer? This is definitely a subject worth exploring. Give your students a breath of fresh prayer.

> ▶ *Advancing the Retreat.* Again, another popular setting for the (literal and figurative) mountaintop spiritual experience. You haul the kids in a van up to a pretty location, then sing songs, play games, eat food, do devotions, watch skits, study the Bible, and so on, and so on, and so on. It's new for kids who have never done it. But is it really a life-changing experience? It can be.

▶ *Concussion Enders for Discussion Starters.* You can find a great variety of discussion starters on the bookshelf. They're great—use them! But sometimes you need to venture into uncharted territory to address the individual needs of your youth group. How can you get students' brains churning in an experiential way?

> ⓓ *Pop Culture Power Tools.* Virtually all teenagers connect with popular culture in one form or another. Whether it's TV, movies, video games, music, magazines, the Internet, or other media, students give their attention. Good or bad, it can be used as a tool. It can be used creatively to make some of the most memorable, life-changing messages teenagers will ever hear.

▶ *To Preach or Not to Preach.* Much research suggests that the majority of traditional preaching can (gasp) go in one ear and out the other. I'm not down-playing preaching, but does *your* preaching truly help students grow in their relationship with Jesus? How does it help them remember God's Word for the rest of their lives? It definitely can, if you think of a fascinating way to do it.

▶ *Partnering With the Whole Church.* Alas, this is a sore point with many youth workers. Does it have to be? Despite the horror stories, you can find plenty of examples of youth ministries working in harmony with the rest of their church body. It can prove to be challenging, no doubt, but it's worthwhile. You just have to find creative solutions.

> ⓓ *Parents Are People Too.* Another bone of contention with tens of thousands of youth workers: Why are some parents so supportive and helpful, while a few seem to behave more as your opponents? Again, creative solutions await you.

● *Fund-raisers Can Be Your Friends.* Making money for your youth ministry is one of the most dreaded ministry areas of all. But if you want to go on that mission trip or need equipment that's not in the budget, raising funds becomes necessary. It can be fun, and it can make you more cash than you might have expected. The Bank of Creativity is now open for business.

## Holy Wow Mix-n-Match

| *Ministry Experiences* | *Creative Tools* |
|---|---|
| ⊙ Bible Lessons | ▫ 4x4 Diary |
| ⊙ Devotions | ▫ 'Zine Zymurgy |
| ⊙ Alternative Worship | ▫ Fruit Salad |
| ⊙ Games | ▫ What Would Snoopy Do? |
| ⊙ Skits | ▫ Alpha-Best |
| ⊙ Outreach | ▫ World Records |
| ⊙ Short-term Missions | ▫ Meta-4s |
| ⊙ Prayer | ▫ Finger Foils |
| ⊙ Retreats | ▫ Bookworms |
| ⊙ Discussion Starters | ▫ Triple Jump |
| ⊙ Pop Culture | ▫ MOAN—Mother of All Nags |
| ⊙ Preaching | ▫ Redefinition |
| ⊙ Partnering With the Whole Church | ▫ Brain Train |
| ⊙ Parents | ▫ Buck-an-Ear |
| ⊙ Fund-raisers | ▫ Popping Opposites |

*Detailed instructions for each of these exercises can be found on the following pages.*

## CREATIVE TOOL 1

### 4x4 Diary

**Materials Needed:** Notebook or journal, pen
**Estimated Time:** Twenty minutes per day for four days

1. Decide on a youth ministry experience you'd like to generate ideas for. In two or three paragraphs, describe how you conducted that activity the last time you did it. Be as specific as you can with the details, including time, setting, people involved, items used, and so on.

2. Read the descriptions of the following fictional teenagers.

   ▫ *Megan* is your angel teenager. Always inclusive of other students, especially new ones. Always positive and optimistic. Always helpful and encouraging. However, her biblical knowledge is weak. She has a pure servant's heart, but it would take her awhile to search for the book of Hezekiah in her little pink Bible.

- *Derek* is a good kid who doesn't ever get in trouble. He'll do whatever you tell him to do. But he's more interested in charming the girls than anything else. He's grown up in the church and has heard all the Bible stories a thousand times, so he's not so sure he has anything else to learn.

- *Kirsten* comes to church because her parents make her. Once she gets in your youth group, her attitude and body language make it very clear she'd rather be somewhere else. She tries to stay on the sidelines. You're not sure what her spiritual life is like because she'll never talk to you.

- *Jeremy*—here comes trouble. You struggle with disappointment when he shows up. He thinks he's cooler than anybody else, always has a smirk on his face, and he might be under the influence of something half the time he's there. At times you've thought about kicking him out, but he doesn't actually do anything wrong. He wouldn't know a Bible from a banana.

**3.** Pretend these four teenagers were among the students who participated in the activity you described in step 1. From the perspective of each of the four teenagers, write a journal entry as described below:

- *Day one:* Write a five-minute entry (one from each teenager's perspective) about what it's like experiencing your activity. Write in the present tense, as if they're experiencing it and writing it in the moment. Convey their honest attitudes and perspectives.

- *Day two:* Write a five-minute entry (for each teenager) about what they might be thinking of your activity the day after. They've had some time to let it sink in. Do they act on it? Do their opinions change? Do they even care? Have each person write at least one way he or she thinks it could have been better.

**4.** Now take your experience from step one and change it. Write one creative change for each of the following characteristics of the activity: setting, how the students interact with the activity, how the students interact with each other, and at least one physical object. Add one element: Now, you talk one-on-one with each teenager about the experience.

**5.** From each teenager's perspective, write new journal entries according to the following instructions:

- *Day three:* All students come back the next week, and this time they experience the same activity, but with the changes you incorporated. Write this day's journal entry as their experiences of it.

- *Day four:* It's the day after. Write journal entries about what each student feels about the previous day's activity and about the interaction with you. Whether they liked it or not, have each teenager make one suggestion for how it could have been more worthwhile.

6. Consider the following:

- Do you think personal interaction with the students would make a difference in their experience? Why or why not?

- After writing and rereading the teenagers' suggestions for making the activity better, what do you think would be one more thing you could change to make the activity fascinating?

- How much did the teenagers *experience* during the activity versus discussion and listening? If they could have experienced the biblical principles you were talking about, what would they have done differently?

**Take It Deeper:** Ask a handful of your real-life students to write short journals about their experiences in your youth group. Have them write a three-part journal: (1) the day of the experience, (2) the day after the experience, and (3) one week later. Ask them to write honestly what they felt they learned from the experience, and have them each make at least one suggestion for making it better. Have them type their responses on a computer so they can stay anonymous and be more honest in their answers. ⊡

# CREATIVE TOOL 2

## 'Zine Zymurgy
**Materials Needed:** A stack of a variety of magazines
**Estimated Time:** Thirty to sixty minutes

This activity works if you do it alone, but it works even better with one or two partners.

1. Decide on a youth ministry experience you'd like to generate ideas for.

2. Read through each advertisement in your magazines as if it were an ad for your ministry experience. Some ads will work great; some of them won't be as strong. For each ad, consider the following questions:

- How would you change the headline to apply to your event?

- How would you change the images to apply to your event?

- What would your "call to action" be on this ad?

- How would your ad emphasize building a relationship with Jesus?

- How would you adjust your ministry activity based on what the ad promised to deliver?

3. Write down the ad concepts that give you and your partner(s) the

strongest reactions. Try to shoot for at least an hour of generating ideas for your ministry experience.

**For example,** let's say you're generating ideas for an alternative worship experience. An ad for an SUV might emphasize the vehicle's power, endurance, and ability to climb the toughest mountains. You might change the ad to talk about a worship experience that strengthens teenagers' power, endurance, and ability to climb the highest mountains. The SUV's image would be a shiny truck on top of a rugged hill. Your alternative worship ad might picture a few rugged teenagers on their knees in prayer on that same mountain. A call to action for the SUV would invite you to come for a test drive. Your ad might ask them to drive to meet you somewhere. The SUV ad might also spark new ideas to make the worship experience itself more memorable, such as doing the activity inside a car or driving the car inside the church to dramatically illustrate a Bible point. ⊡

## CREATIVE TOOL 3

### Fruit Salad

**Materials Needed:** Fruit salad ingredients, pen, paper
**Estimated Time:** One hour

Do this activity with one or two partners.

1. Decide on a youth ministry experience you'd like to generate ideas for.

2. Gather together all your ingredients for your fruit salad, including several varieties of fruit; some kind of yogurt, cream, or juice; and whatever else you'd like to put in your fruit salad (you may want to be creative and find a fancy, complex recipe).

3. Have one of your partners take notes as you all participate in the discussion. As you make the fruit salad together, consider the following questions.

⊡ Take five full minutes to think of at least thirty different varieties of fruit salad. Have your recorder write them all down. You can make them up; they don't have to be real. (This part of the activity clears your head and gets your mind sparking.)

⊡ Think about your youth ministry challenge. You're all making fruit salad. As you're washing the fruit, think of at least twenty different things your teenagers could *make* during your activity. Have your recorder write them all down.

⊡ As you're cutting up the fruit, think of at least twenty different excuses your teenagers could have for "cutting out" and not participating in your activity. Write them all down.

- As you add various ingredients to your fruit salad, think of at least twenty different physical objects from a teenager's life you could add to make the activity more relevant to their lives. Write them down.

- As you mix all the ingredients together, think of at least twenty ways you could have students interact with each other during the activity. Write them down.

- As you eat your fruit salad, review your lists of ideas and talk about how some of them might work together to form a memorable, holy wow experience that brings your teenagers closer to Jesus.

**Connect It to Your Youth:** Do this activity with a small group of teenagers. Instead of trying to solve a youth ministry problem, choose a relevant biblical topic to discuss as you make your fruit salad together. Ask the students questions as you do each part of the process. Create your own questions based on your individual teenagers' experiences. ·

## CREATIVE TOOL 4

### What Would Snoopy Do?

**Materials Needed:** Pen, paper
**Estimated Time:** Thirty to sixty minutes

Do this activity with one or two partners.

1. Decide on a youth ministry experience you'd like to generate ideas for.

2. Choose a specific theme you'd like to revolve this experience around (such as forgiveness, authority, or sexual purity).

3. Have each participant (including yourself) write a list of each of your top five (for a thirty-minute exercise) or top ten (for a sixty-minute exercise) favorite fictional characters. They can be any character you choose, from Bugs Bunny to Barbie to Frodo Baggins. Be sure to get a wide variety of fictional characters.

4. Consider the following questions for each character:

- What would be this character's response in a situation that involved this topic? (For example, how would Snoopy forgive somebody?)

- What would be this character's most memorable experience in church?

- How would this character use his or her favorite object as a metaphor for this topic?

- In which setting would this character be most comfortable talking about his or her relationship with Jesus?

- How would this character suggest you conduct your ministry experience?

5. Review your answers together. If you can think of additional relevant questions, go ahead and ask them. Consider these additional questions:

- In what ways are your fictional characters' responses similar to what your teenagers might say? How are they different?

- Pick two or three suggestions from your characters' ideas that might be viable with teenagers. How might you adjust these activities to make them more memorable for your students?

## CREATIVE TOOL 5

### Alpha-Best

**Materials Needed:** Pen, paper, a one- or two-minute timer, several copies of the page "Alpha-Best List" (p. 135)
**Estimated Time:** Thirty to sixty minutes

Do this activity with one or two partners.

1. Decide on a youth ministry experience you'd like to generate ideas for.

2. Randomly pick a letter of the alphabet—except Q, U, V, X, Y or Z.

3. Within the allotted time, write down one response to each category on the "Alpha-Best List," using the chosen letter of the alphabet. (For example, if the letter is "A," and the category is "Things You Pray For," you might write "aunts" or "ailments.") If you get stuck on one, go to the next one.

4. Share your answers, then select a new letter and repeat step 3.

5. After you've created at least three lists (with three different letters), consider the following:

- How do any of the answers present interesting ideas or viable options?

- Mix and match your answers. What might your youth ministry experience look like if you included some of these ideas together?

- Discuss with your partners some general ideas for your proposed ministry experience. Use the words you've generated to spark your thinking.

- The timer is designed to force quick, spontaneous answers. If you can't generate enough answers in that time, feel free to extend your time limit or do the activity aloud together with your group.

- Create a list of twelve categories that relate specifically to your church or youth group. Do the activity again, this time looking for ideas that can be customized to your unique situation.

## Alpha-Best List 1

**Letter Choice:** _____    **Letter Choice:** _____    **Letter Choice:** _____

1. Things You Pray For
2. Names for Christ
3. Good Character Traits
4. Items in a Sanctuary
5. Worship Song Titles
6. Things We Treasure
7. Sins
8. Things Friends Do Together
9. Things We Never Forget
10. Items Students Carry to School
11. Words Associated With Pain
12. Things Teenagers Eat

## Alpha-Best List 2

**Letter Choice:** _____    **Letter Choice:** _____    **Letter Choice:** _____

1. Names of Bible Characters
2. Clothes Teenagers Wear
3. Things We Judge People For
4. Words Associated With Love
5. Kinds of Relationships
6. Terms of Endearment
7. Things We Do When We're Bored
8. Beverages Teenagers Drink
9. Things That Make Us Angry
10. Ways to Die
11. Things That Grow
12. Places Teenagers Hang Out

# CREATIVE TOOL 6

## World Records

**Materials Needed:** Pen, paper, *Guinness Book of World Records* (if possible)

**Estimated Time:** Twenty to thirty minutes

This exercise can be done alone, but it works better with a small group.

1. Decide on a youth ministry experience you'd like to generate ideas for.

2. Write a list of attributes for that specific experience. For example, for a short-term mission trip, you might write some of the following words: *travel, witnessing, food delivery, repairs, driving for hours, sleeping bags, toothbrushes,* and so on.

3. With or without the aid of the *Guinness Book of World Records,* talk about what some of those elements would be like if you were to set world records with them. Don't worry about being realistic or actually setting records—that's not the point of the activity. For example, what if you set the record for delivering the world's largest bag of dried pinto beans? Or you set the record for the longest continuous road-trip song?

4. Be as wild and out of the ordinary as you can. Force yourself or your group to think of at least twenty-five possible world records.

5. Talk about your list. None of the items are likely to be possible. But what would your activity be like if you toned it back a bit? Instead of trying to set a world record, you actually did something highly exaggerated.

6. Consider the following questions:

   - What would your experience be like if you actually did the "exaggerated" (not the world record) version of the activity?

   - How would doing it this way make the experience memorable?

   - In what ways could you reinforce teenagers' relationship with Jesus?

   - How might this exaggerated experience help students remember and apply Scripture? ⋅


# CREATIVE TOOL 7

## Meta-4s

**Materials Needed:** Pen, paper, four different sales catalogs (any type), a clock

**Estimated Time:** Thirty to sixty minutes

This exercise can be done alone, but it works better with a small group.

1. Decide on a youth ministry experience or study topic you'd like to generate ideas for.

2. Each participant takes a catalog and pages through it for four minutes. During that four minutes, try to find four metaphors for your selected ministry experience or study topic. Look carefully for details. Even a clothes catalog may have a variety of potential metaphors such as stitches, hems, buttons, hair, or pockets, as well as abstract concepts such as beauty, posing, friendship, or health. Don't think too deeply about what those metaphors might mean—just look for concepts that might have a connection. Write down the four key words or phrases.

3. After four minutes, switch catalogs and repeat step 2. Do this for all four catalogs.

4. Combine your lists of metaphors and discuss the deeper meaning of each one as it relates to your experience or topic. Talk about how that might apply to the lives of teenagers in a memorable and intriguing way.

5. Choose one or two strong metaphors that have potential to be developed into a holy wow experience that will bring teenagers closer in their relationship with Jesus. ⊡

# CREATIVE TOOL 8

## Finger Foils

**Materials Needed:** Paper, scissors, colored pencils or markers, tape
**Estimated Time:** Twenty to thirty minutes

This exercise can be done alone, but it works better with a partner.

1. Decide on a youth ministry experience or study topic.

2. Make a creative finger puppet of yourself and one or two teenagers that would be representative of a type of teenager in your group. If you choose a specific person, remain respectful of that person and do the activity in private.

3. Using the puppets, act out your potential experience or topical discussion between the two "actors." This may seem silly, but it actually works because it weakens your inhibitions about the problem and prevents you from becoming too "left-brained" about your approach. Push yourself to extend the conversation for at least ten minutes. Time yourself, if necessary.

4. Have the puppets ask probing questions, such as, "Why do we have to learn this lesson in the first place?" or "Why can't you pay more attention?" Be loose and a little goofy, but make sure your answers are entirely honest.

5. Write down key observations about what your puppets have said, even

things you wouldn't have said in real life.

**6.** Consider the following questions:

- In what ways would a finger puppet conversation be different from the real thing? How would it be similar?

- Are there things about your pretend conversation that should be applied to your real-life experience or topic?

- Some people oppose the concept of role-playing. How else might you help teenagers experience what it's like to talk with Jesus?

**Connect It to Your Youth:** If done right (and not in a childish way), these finger puppet discussions can also help youth sort out certain issues with each other. They'll be tempted to do nothing but be goofy with them, but when you begin to ask serious questions, they'll find they can be more honest about the issue because they're projecting their thoughts through the objects. They'll still feel safe while having the freedom to speak truthfully. ·

## CREATIVE TOOL 9

### Bookworms

**Materials Needed:** Two or more youth ministry idea books (see Appendix 1 for some examples), pen, paper

**Estimated Time:** Thirty to sixty minutes

**1.** Decide on a youth ministry experience or study topic you'd like to generate ideas for.

**2.** Choose two or more youth ministry idea books. Pick a random number—this number will be the page number you refer to in both books.

**3.** Read through the text, questions, and activities on that page in each of the books. Ask yourself what an experience might be like if you combined the thoughts and/or elements from the two separate books. Think about how an activity in one book might provide an interesting twist on the thoughts in another book. Write down any observations you make.

**4.** Pick a new number and repeat step 3 several times. Give yourself a time goal—push yourself to go for at least thirty minutes.

**Take It Deeper:** Instead of using youth ministry books, you can look for examples, illustrations, and new ideas in fiction books. This exercise is more useful for finding ideas for study topics.

**1.** Decide on a relevant study topic you'd like to generate ideas for.

**2.** Select two to four fiction books; it doesn't matter if you've read them before.

**3.** Choose a random page number in any book and read through that page. Do you see any potential connections or illustrations in that section that might tie in to your topic? If so, write them down and think about them further. If not, pick a new page number and do it again.

**4.** Repeat this process at least twenty times. The more you look, the more likely you'll find a new connection. The key to the success of this exercise is to commit to a time goal—work at least thirty minutes or longer to search for ideas. ⊡

# CREATIVE TOOL 10

## Triple Jump

**Materials Needed:** Notepad, pen
**Estimated Time:** Twenty to forty minutes

This idea works well either alone or with a small group.

**1.** Decide on a youth ministry experience you'd like to generate ideas for.

**2.** Turn your notepad to a horizontal position. On the lower left side of your paper, write the name of the experience you want to do (for example, "outreach approach"). On the lower right side of your paper, write your goal (for example, "Give my teenagers an opportunity to share their faith").

**3.** Draw a straight line between the two points. On that line, write a basic idea for how you normally would get from your experience to the goal. For example, for an outreach experience with a goal of helping teenagers share their faith, you might write, "Have students distribute brochures in public."

**4.** Next draw a higher, curved line that "jumps" over the other line. On this line write an idea that's more innovative. It may still be safe and easy, but it should be a better idea. This is your first jump.

**5.** Now draw a higher line that "jumps" over the first two lines. Write an idea that's a bit wilder, more risky, more adventurous, and more inventive. This is your second jump.

**6.** Draw a fourth line that "jumps" over all the others. The ideas you write on this line should be highly imaginative, bold, over the top, maybe even a little crazy. This is your third jump. This is where you'll find your holy wow experience. Remember, it's easy to tame an idea that's a bit too wild.

**7.** Start over and do the triple jump at least five times, starting with a basic, average idea and "leaping" until you think of the most original and unforgettable idea for each third jump. ⊡

# CREATIVE TOOL 11

## MOAN—Mother of All Nags

**Materials Needed:** Notepad, pen, photo of a "nagging" mother figure (optional)

**Estimated Time:** Twenty to forty minutes

This idea works best with a small group.

1. Decide on a youth ministry experience you'd like to generate ideas for.

2. Take two minutes and drain your brain of all the ideas you've already had in mind for this experience—any preconceptions, existing ideas or expectations. Write them all down on paper as quickly as you can.

3. Have each participant (including yourself) describe what they picture a "nagging mother" to be like. Take turns sharing an experience when you've been nagged by someone else. Have fun with it, and use voices if you're so inclined. If you're uncomfortable using a mother figure for this exercise, use a different nagging character.

4. Take a look at the list of ideas you wrote down in step 2. Have each participant evaluate that idea from the perspective of their "nag." Think of all the possible things that could go wrong with that idea, why it couldn't possibly work, and other contentions, such as

- "Nobody wants to do that. I'll tell you why…"

- "Somebody's going to get hurt. Don't you realize…"

- "Whoever heard of such dumb ideas! Why, when I was a kid…"

- This will never work. For one thing…"

Think of as many objections as possible, and keep "nagging" for at least fifteen minutes. Write them all down.

5. After your nagging session, talk about why some of those objections actually make your idea better. For example, one objection might be that teenagers would never talk about a certain subject. Think about why the opposite might be true and how you would go about stimulating such a conversation.

6. Develop new ideas based on the "nagging" objections. Use them as a springboard for making them actually work. ⊡

# CREATIVE TOOL 12

## Redefinition

**Materials Needed:** Notepad, pen, dictionary, thesaurus
**Estimated Time:** Thirty to forty-five minutes

This idea can work for you alone, but it works better with a partner or two.

1. Choose a youth ministry activity or topic.

2. Write down a commonly accepted definition of the subject you've chosen. You might look it up in the dictionary, but try to come up with your own specific definition.

3. Take each word in the definition and replace it with a synonym. Write a parallel definition with all new words. If possible, write up to five definitions using all different synonyms for each word.

4. Now take your original definition and redefine it from these viewpoints:

- A pastor
- A teenager
- An eighty-year-old
- A five-year-old
- An atheist or agnostic
- Jesus Christ

5. Now take your original definition and redefine it in different contexts:

- In a school
- At a ballgame
- At a rock concert
- At a mall or lifestyle center
- In a restaurant or coffeehouse
- At a gym or health center

Challenge yourself to rethink the activity to make it fit, even if it becomes absurd or unlikely.

6. Review your various definitions and consider these questions:

- How do different perspectives change the nature of the subject?
- In different contexts, how much does the nature and purpose of the subject change? How can it still be a spiritual experience in those contexts?
- How could you apply some of these definitions to your youth group?

# CREATIVE TOOL 13

## Brain Train

**Materials Needed:** Long sheets of paper, pen
**Estimated Time:** Thirty to sixty minutes

This idea works alone, but it works better with a small group.

1. Decide on a youth ministry activity you'd like to generate ideas for.

2. Write your activity in a box on the left side of a long, horizontal sheet of paper.

3. Have one participant think of the first three things that come to mind when thinking about that concept. For example, when someone thinks of worship, the words *music, raised hands,* and *God* might come up. Write down those three words or phrases in the next "train car"—a box to the right of your first box.

4. Choose one of those new three words. Have the next participant think of the first three things that come to mind when thinking of the newly chosen word. Write those new three words in a box to the right of your previous box.

5. Continue around your group in the same manner, choosing a word from the set of three words and spontaneously thinking of three new words.

6. After extending your "train" out to eight or ten "cars," review the words on the list and look for ideas and connections that might make your ministry activity more memorable. Be open to words that might spark a new way to experience God's truth.

7. Start new trains and repeat steps 3 through 6. Commit to developing and discussing each train for at last fifteen minutes. Push your group to develop at least three or four trains. ⊡

# CREATIVE TOOL 14

## Buck-an-Ear

**Materials Needed:** Notepad, pen, a handful of one-dollar bills
**Estimated Time:** Sixty to ninety minutes

This idea works well either alone or with a partner.

1. Select a youth ministry experience or study topic.

2. Write out a short list of questions you would ask somebody about your objective. You're going to be talking with people who are not in youth ministry, maybe not even in the church. Make sure your questions are provocative and open-ended enough to elicit a worthwhile response. Don't ask questions that can be answered yes or no. Try to be specific in your questions,

especially as they relate to your local community.

**3.** Find at least ten people to interview. Tell them you'll give them a dollar if they'll give you a few minutes of their time. If you talk to people you don't know, be sure to tell them who you are and what you do. You're looking for fresh perspectives. Be sure to write down their responses.

**4.** After your interviews, review your notes with a partner. Look for new ideas, connections, and viewpoints you never considered before. How would some of those new ideas look if you experienced them with your youth group?

**Alternative Option:** "Rabbit Ears" is a variation of this same exercise. Instead of offering a dollar or taking notes, have a partner videotape your interviewees' comments, then review their responses later. The on-camera approach puts people in a different mind-set and will sometimes encourage them to say things they wouldn't say otherwise. ⊡

# CREATIVE TOOL 15

## Popping Opposites
**Materials Needed:** Notepad, pen
**Estimated Time:** Twenty to forty minutes

This idea works well either alone or with a small group.

**1.** Decide on a youth ministry activity you'd like to generate ideas for.

**2.** On the left-hand side of your paper, write as many adjectives and verbs as you can think of to describe that specific activity. Consider all of its elements—the audience, setting, timing, types of objects used, action, and so on. For example, for a worship experience, you might write some of the following words: *sing, kneel, flowing, intimate, quiet, dance,* or *low-lit.* Push yourself to think of at least fifty descriptive words.

**3.** On the right-hand side of your paper, write at least two or three opposites for each descriptive word. These can be contradictions, inverses, antonyms, comparisons—anything that's very different from the original word.

**4.** What might the activity look like if these were the words you were using to describe that experience? How could you create a memorable experience by doing the polar opposite of what you originally thought?

**Take It Deeper:** Create an experience using the first list of words. Then, a week later, create the opposite experience. Don't tell your students what you're doing. Instead, closely observe their reactions to each method. Hear what they're saying (and not saying), perceive their emotional responses, and evaluate how the two different experiences might strengthen their relationships with Jesus in different ways. ⊡

# ~~Chapter 16~~

## Bent on Jesus

Is your ministry, right now, living out precisely the way you expected it to five years ago? Even one year ago? Not likely.

If you're living your life biblically, you're letting God guide you as you grow in your relationship with him. Being able to trust God in that way means we give up any effort at predicting what's going to happen next.

As much as we try to plot out the course of our lives (personally and professionally) with straight, defined lines, we know those lines will get messed up. Although the indelible past is inked forever, the future's a dull pencil with a giant eraser.

This doesn't mean that life becomes "carefree"; rather, it requires that we live by the substance of faith and hope. Many of us are driven by what's possible—and we want God to surprise us. So we organize, we prepare, we anticipate, and we're proactive. But the best-laid plans often take unexpected turns.

### Be Ye Diagonal

How do you choose a direction for your youth ministry?

There's horizontal. There's vertical.

Then there's everything else.

You can lean. You can bend. You can go slanted, curved, wavy, angled, or slope style. Just don't be conformed…renew your mind…and be transformed. The "straight and narrow" is referring to biblical obedience, not your creativity.

Perhaps the ultimate question to ask yourself is this: Is my youth ministry really working? Horizontal is flat and gives you no momentum. Vertical is an impossible climb or a straight drop. Engaging youth with a real, growing fascination with Jesus gives you every angle possible.

The answers are, of course, entirely up to you. As long as your response includes an unwavering devotion to obeying God, the rest is wide open.

## The Beginning

This is not the end. This is where we start. The story has yet to be told—and lived. The Spirit is leading the way, your brain is dutifully waiting to be sparked, and your teenagers are ready to be fascinated.

All you need now is a little creativity.

Or a lot. That's up to you.

# Appendix

## Appendix 1: Recommended Idea Books

Often the best place to get your creativity juices flowing is with existing youth ministry idea books and kits. Here are some great ones from Group Publishing (in alphabetical order).

- *Christ In Me: 30 Next-Level Encounters*
- *Creative Faith Ah-Ha's!* by Thom & Joani Schultz
- *Discovering Jesus: A Multimedia Journey*
- *Meet Jesus*
- *Faith Metaphors: 50 Interactive Object Lessons for Youth Ministry*
- *Group's Blockbuster Movie Illustrations—The Sequel* by Bryan Belknap
- *Morph!* by Ron Martoia
- *No More Lone Rangers* by David Chow
- *The Prayer Path: A Christ-Centered Labyrinth Experience*
- *The Preteen Worker's Encyclopedia of Bible-Teaching Ideas*
- *UnLearning Church* by Mike Slaughter
- *An Unstoppable Force* by Erwin McManus
- *Why Nobody Learns Much of Anything at Church: And How to Fix It* by Thom & Joani Schultz
- *Walking in His Footsteps: a Multimedia Journey Through Jesus' Last Week*
- *Worshipmania: 80 Active Worship Experiences for Young Teenagers*

## Appendix 2: Recommended Reading

It would be easy to recommend a variety of good books on creativity. However, usually when I see a list of related or recommended resources at the back of a book, I don't read any of them. So I won't give you an exhaustive list.

Instead, here are *three of the best books* you'll ever find on the subject of creativity. If you read them, they'll likely make your short list of all-time favorites.

- *Walking on Water* by Madeleine L'Engle
- *Orbiting the Giant Hairball* by Gordon MacKenzie
- *Journey of the Imagination* by Renwick St. James and James Christensen

Fiction can often give us a deeper and even more memorable portrayal of creativity. Here are a couple of stirring novels I highly recommend.

- *My Name Is Asher Lev* by Chaim Potok
- *A Severed Wasp* by Madeleine L'Engle

I also recommend these very useful books to keep in your personal library to help spark your imagination. They're all available at amazon.com or bn.com.
- Anything by Dr. Seuss
- DK (Dorling Kindersley) books (www.dk.com)
- Klutz books (www.klutz.com)
- *Roget's International Thesaurus*
- *The Stinky Cheese Man and Other Fairly Stupid Tales* by John Scieszka and Lane Smith
- *The New Comprehensive American Rhyming Dictionary* by Sue Young
- *Random House Webster's Word Menu* by Stephen Glazier

## Appendix 3: Recommended Play—A "Cata-List"

Here's a list of items that can help you get more oil for your lamp. Collect them over time and store them in an accessible cabinet or plastic storage bin.
- ○ Loads of scrap paper
- ○ Plastic building blocks and connectable toys
- ○ Modeling clay
- ○ Blank journals
- ○ Colored index cards
- ○ Colored sticky notes—all sizes
- ○ Board game letter tiles (at least two sets)
- ○ Marbles
- ○ Stress balls
- ○ Construction paper
- ○ Plain wooden blocks (you'll want to write on them)
- ○ Foam balls, tennis balls, rubber balls
- ○ Rope and string
- ○ Colored chalk
- ○ Glue sticks and hot glue
- ○ Candy
- ○ Darts
- ○ Sound effects CDs
- ○ Pipe cleaners
- ○ Instant camera and film
- ○ A variety of containers
- ○ Magazines
- ○ Photographer and illustrator directories (they're free—ask a graphic designer for old copies)
- ○ Paint and fabric swatches

# Scripture Index

Refer to this index to find biblical support for the ideas presented in this book.